01 Introduction

02 Chapter 1: Credit Counseling

06 Chapter 2: Chapter 7 vs Chapter 13

09 Chapter 3: Where to Find Bankruptcy Forms Online

25 Chapter 4: Being Judgment Proof

31 Chapter 5: BE Adviser – Debtor Education

40 Chapter 6: BK Filter

42 Chapter 7: UpSolve

46 Chapter 8: Bankruptcy Courts

52 Conclusion

55 References

57 Appendices

© Copyright 2019 by BE Adviser, LLC - All rights reserved.

The following guide is reproduced below with the goal of providing information that is as accurate and reliable as possible. Regardless, purchasing this guide can be seen as consent to the fact that both the publisher and the author of this book are in no way experts on the topics discussed within and that any recommendations or suggestions that are made herein are for entertainment purposes only. Professionals should be consulted as needed before undertaking any of the action endorsed herein.

This declaration is deemed fair and valid by both the American Bar Association and the Committee of Publishers Association and is legally binding throughout the United States.

Furthermore, the transmission, duplication, or reproduction of any of the following work including specific information will be considered an illegal act irrespective of if it is done electronically or in print. This extends to creating a secondary or tertiary copy of the work or a recorded copy and is only allowed with the express written consent from the Publisher. All additional right reserved.

The information in the following pages is broadly considered a truthful and accurate account of facts and as such, any inattention, use, or misuse of the information in question by the reader will render any resulting actions solely under their purview. There are no scenarios in which the publisher or the original author of this work can be in any fashion deemed liable for any hardship or damages that may befall them after undertaking information described herein.

Additionally, the information in the following pages is intended only for informational purposes and should thus be thought of as universal. As befitting its nature, it is presented without assurance regarding its prolonged validity or interim quality. Trademarks that are mentioned are done without written consent and can in no way be considered an endorsement from the trademark holder.

INTRODUCTION

We've created a budget, and, more importantly, stuck to it. We have an emergency fund and other liquid assets. But the bills are getting out of control. Medical emergencies, car problems, student loans, overspending on holidays and vacations are all starting to weigh on our shoulders.

Then, the unexpected, worst thing possible happens – we lose our job. Our household is short one income – the income that helped pay for the overspending and vacations. We blow through our emergency fund in just a couple of weeks because we never really added to it every month like we should have. Our credit cards are maxed out. We are on the verge of foreclosure. Is there anything we can do?

There is: filing bankruptcy. Bankruptcy is a way to relieve you of debt while protecting the assets you need to keep. For instance, student loans cannot be discharged in bankruptcy; therefore, you will still be paying on them after your bankruptcy is discharged. You can also take a step called reaffirming. This means you keep certain things – like a house and cars – out of the bankruptcy and keep paying on them.

You might think, "Well, we blew it! We're filing bankruptcy and we can't let anyone know!" Believe it or not, the number of consumers filing bankruptcy in this country between 2006 and 2017 was more than 12.7 million (United States, 2018). So, if you find yourself in this type of position, you are not alone – not by a long shot.

In this text we will learn about credit counseling, the types of bankruptcy available to consumers, filing online, becoming judgment proof, and some of the resources available to anyone needing advice on filing bankruptcy.

FILE BANKRUPTCY FOR FREE

CHAPTER 1
CREDIT COUNSELING

Before you take the step of actually filing for bankruptcy, there are two other options you can pursue: consolidating debt and selling off assets.

If you are close to filing bankruptcy, it may be too late for consolidating debt as the banks probably won't approve such a loan. You may have already sold off your assets to stay afloat as long as possible, so that option may also not exist.

So, before you file for bankruptcy, you must complete credit counseling. As of 2005, credit counseling became a requirement before filing for bankruptcy. "Pre-bankruptcy credit counseling, also known as the pre-filing course, is something that you will be legally required to do if you ever have to file for bankruptcy. This requirement was mandated in 2005 when the Bankruptcy Abuse Prevention and Consumer Protection Act was signed into law by President George W. Bush" (CC, Pre, 2018).

There are dozens of sites on the internet that offer advice and credit counseling. However, the advisors at **CC Advising (ccadvising.com)** are United States Trustee approved counselors who offer the courses you are required to take. Once you complete the first course, The First Bankruptcy Course, you will receive a certificate good for 180 days to provide to the court or your attorney of record (CC, Ultimate, 2018).

What is the purpose of Credit Counseling?

During Credit Counseling, you will review your financial situation with a certified credit counselor. They review your debt to income ratio, your budget, your assets and debts, and review any and all alternatives to resolve your debt issues without filing bankruptcy. Specifically, the counselor will use the analysis of your current financial situation, discuss the factors that contributed to that financial situation, and help in developing a plan to take action on those financial problems (CC, Ultimate, 2018)

How long does the counseling session generally take?

You need to go at your own pace so that you are certain you understand everything in one module before moving on to the next. Most clients take somewhere between 60 to 90 minutes to complete the session, but it varies depending on your particular situation (CC, Ultimate, 2018).

What information do I need to take the course?

You will need documentation of your income and monthly budget expenses, your current debts, why you sought counseling, information about any lawsuits, garnishments, or foreclosures you may be facing, and any assets you may have. There is no section of the course that requires you to have exact amounts, so you can estimate. But, be accurate. The counselors are making decisions and giving advice based on the numbers you provide (CC, Ultimate, 2018).

You Must Take Credit Counseling from an Approved Provider

You can only take the credit counseling course from an approved, nonprofit provider. CC Advising (ccadvising.com) is approved in all U.S. States and territories, but not every provider is, so you need to verify whether the provider you choose is approved, either by the US Trustee's office or by the Bankruptcy Administrators (in Alabama and North Carolina) (CC, Ultimate, 2018).

How can I find my Court District?

Your attorney can provide you with your court district location. You can also try calling the Bankruptcy Court and asking (also, see Appendix B).

What types of subjects does the CC Advising credit counseling session cover?

- Introduction
- Reasons for Seeking Counseling
- Reasons for Seeking Credit Counseling Explained
- Debt Structure
- Budget
- Budget Chart and Analysis
- Debt-to-Income Ratio
- Alternatives to Bankruptcy
- Consumer Laws
- Rebuilding Credit After Bankruptcy
- Identity Check
- Chat with a Credit Counselor

Why do I have to fill out a budget?

The credit counselor uses your budget to determine whether you have options other than bankruptcy available to resolve your debt issues. They will give you tips and tricks to stay out of debt and put you on the path to solvency. Your credit counselor is looking for a snapshot of your financial situation before you meet with an attorney (CC, Ultimate, 2018).

 ### Will my attorney or bankruptcy court accept your certificate?

Yes, of course. The certificate you receive after completing the CC Advising credit counseling course is accepted everywhere, by all attorneys and by all bankruptcy courts (CC, Ultimate, 2018).

 ### How long is my certificate good for?

Since the certificate lasts 180 days (about six months), this step is one you just want to get out of the way before you contact an attorney or start bankruptcy proceedings. You can always take the credit counseling Pro Se (without an attorney) and find an attorney to file your bankruptcy later (CC, Ultimate 2018). The first step of bankruptcy is credit counseling, and the nice thing about the CC Advising program is you can sign up at ccadvising.com and it is all done online.

Also, just because you take the credit counseling course, it does not mean you have to file bankruptcy. If you later decide bankruptcy is not the solution you wish to pursue, that is absolutely fine. Your completion of a credit counseling course is kept strictly confidential, and it is not reported to the credit bureaus.

FIRST STEP IN BANKRUPTCY
Complete Credit Counseling Online Here:

ccadvising.com

The National Association of Consumer Bankruptcy Attorneys (NACBA's) attorney finder is a great source for finding competent attorneys. Generally, the initial consultation is free, so it makes sense to go visit a few bankruptcy attorneys after you have completed the credit counseling, even if you cannot afford to retain them. They will give you advice and let you know if bankruptcy seems like the best option for your circumstances (National, 2017).

NACBA ATTORNEY FINDER

http://network.nacba.org/advanced-search

One issue NACBA attorneys can advise you on is whether to file Chapter 7 Bankruptcy or Chapter 13 Bankruptcy. Each process varies and which one you use will depend on the number of assets you have, what types of debt you have, and which bankruptcy path will serve you the best.

CHAPTER 2
CHAPTER 7 VS CHAPTER 13

Most consumer bankruptcies are filed under Chapter 7 or Chapter 13. Prior to deciding to start credit counseling, first you must determine your eligibility for filing bankruptcy. "Due to its sweeping relief, Chapter 7 is only available to those debtors with little or no disposable income. Since the vast majority of Chapter 7 debtors receive a discharge, as opposed to having their cases dismissed or forced to switch to Chapter 13, it is clear that the overwhelming majority of people who file Chapter 7 cannot afford to repay their debts" (Nolo, 2019).

If you find yourself ineligible for Chapter 7, "Chapter 13 is entitled Individual Debt Adjustment. It essentially amounts to a repayment plan. The good news is that a Chapter 13 debtor need only pay unsecured creditors what he or she can afford to pay, as long as they receive at least what they would have in a Chapter 7. Unlike credit counseling repayment plans that require the counseling agency to negotiate with creditors, no negotiation is required, and no interest is charged. The balances are fixed at the time of filing" (Nolo, 2019).

CHAPTER 7

Chapter 7 is a liquidation bankruptcy that frees you from most of your unsecured debts, like credit cards and medical bills, without the need to repay. If you want to file Chapter 7 bankruptcy, you must meet income requirements. If you make too much money, you may be required to file another way (O'Neill, 2019).

Once you file for Chapter 7, a court order called the "automatic stay" stops most creditors from continuing collection efforts. Also, you will have a bankruptcy trustee assigned to manage your case. He or she will review your bankruptcy papers and supporting documents. The trustee's job is to sell your nonexempt property (property that you can't protect with a bankruptcy exemption) to pay back your creditors. Should you not have any nonexempt assets, your creditors get nothing (O'Neill, 2019).

Chapter 7 bankruptcy is a good option for low-income debtors with few or no assets. It also works for bankruptcy filers whose "total discharged debt exceeds the value of the property sold—especially if the trustee will apply the funds to non-dischargeable debt, such as income tax or support arrearages" (O'Neill, 2019).

Finding an attorney to help you with your bankruptcy is an important part of the process. If you cannot afford an attorney, you can find the Legal Aid Societies in your state (see Appendix A), find a pro bono attorney, or see if your chosen attorney is willing to negotiate his or her fee (Bulkat, 2019).

If you are wanting to file for bankruptcy yourself, Chapter 7 is definitely the best choice. NOLO, one of the first legal self-help organizations, has a great textbook on filing on your own, How to File for Chapter 7 Bankruptcy. This awesome guide can be purchased at the NOLO website, https://store.nolo.com/products.

How to File for Chapter 7 Bankruptcy gives you what you need to determine whether bankruptcy is right for you:

- which debts get wiped out in bankruptcy
- what property you'll be able to keep (you don't lose everything)
- how to retain your home or car, if possible
- whether your income qualifies you to file for Chapter 7 bankruptcy
- complete the official bankruptcy court forms
- file your debtor education course certificates
- prepare for the meeting of creditors (the one appearance you'll make), and
- rebuild your credit after receiving your fresh start

If your Chapter 7 bankruptcy is simple (meaning that you have little to no income or assets, and there is nothing else that could complicate your bankruptcy), you should be able to file on your own successfully. "But even a simple Chapter 7 bankruptcy requires that you put in a significant amount of time and research. If you are not willing to make the necessary commitment, you risk having your bankruptcy dismissed or putting your property in danger" (Bullkat, 2019).

While you can successfully file Chapter 7 on your own, filing Chapter 13 on your own is not advisable under any circumstances. You should always try to get representation wherever possible. Courts and trustees can be harder on clients representing themselves due to their perceived ignorance of the process.

Even filing Chapter 7 on your own is a bad idea. The American Bankruptcy Institute reports that, "Pro se chapter 7 debtors are nearly 10 times as likely to have their cases dismissed or their discharges denied than debtors with attorneys" (ABI, 2019).

If you are certain you can file Chapter 7 on your own, the remaining chapters of this book will help you with that process.

CHAPTER 13

Chapter 13 is known as a reorganization bankruptcy for debtors with steady income who have enough left over each month to pay back some of their debts through a repayment plan.

In Chapter 13 bankruptcy, you keep all of your property (including nonexempt assets—but you'll have to pay creditors an amount equal to the value of your nonexempt property). In exchange, you pay back all or a portion of your debt through a repayment plan (depending on your income, expenses, and type of debts (O'Neill, 2019).

Chapter 13 bankruptcy is for debtors who

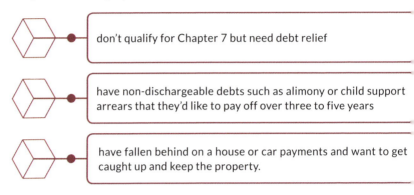

- don't qualify for Chapter 7 but need debt relief
- have non-dischargeable debts such as alimony or child support arrears that they'd like to pay off over three to five years
- have fallen behind on a house or car payments and want to get caught up and keep the property.

But one option that attorneys may push that is not in your best interest is the Fee Only Chapter 13 Bankruptcy plan. "If you can't afford to pay your attorney fee upfront, your lawyer can suggest filing a Chapter 13 bankruptcy (even if you want to file a Chapter 7) for the sole purpose of paying your attorney fees through your repayment plan" (Bulkat, 2019).

Many courts won't allow fee-only Chapter 13 plans; others will consider your overall circumstances when deciding whether or not to approve a fee-only bankruptcy. The reason some courts won't approve it is because it's a borderline unethical way to put a client in a 3-5 year plan and pay twice as much for the bankruptcy because they don't have enough money upfront for a Chapter 7.

Assuming you are eligible and can confidently complete the forms on your own, a Chapter 7 bankruptcy can be done totally for free, without an attorney.

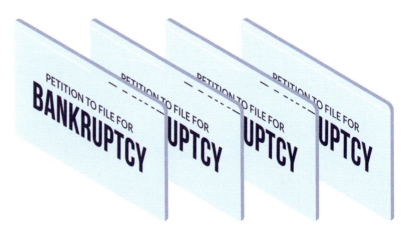

CHAPTER 3
WHERE TO FIND BANKRUPTCY FORMS ONLINE

There are multiple ways to secure the necessary paperwork for filing bankruptcy on your own. However, some of the online options will charge you for access to their software, which includes forms you can get for free from the following sites:

- https://www.uscourts.gov/forms/bankruptcy-forms
- https://www.nolo.com/legal-encyclopedia/forms
- https://upsolve.org/learn/find-free-bankruptcy-chapter7-forms/
- https://wallethub.com/edu/d/filing-bankruptcy-chapter-7/25866/

There are hundreds of websites that claim to offer forms; however, not many of them are truly free. Some will require you to purchase software, legal services, or "packages" of forms that are available for free at the below sites.

USCOURTS.GOV

Not only does this site offer free bankruptcy forms, but it also gives detailed directions on how to fill out the forms properly. This is the best place to get the forms, direct from the official source.

NOLO.GOV

This all-inclusive site gives you the forms as well as dozens of articles on how best to file bankruptcy without an attorney, the differences between Chapter 7 and Chapter 13, and offers manuals for sale on how to file for bankruptcy.

UPSOLVE.ORG

Just like nolo.org, Upsolve is a comprehensive website for the consumer who needs to file for bankruptcy without an attorney. The site offers forms as well as a learning center to educate consumers prior to filing for bankruptcy.

WALLETHUB.COM

Wallet Hub is a great financial website for many financial issues. The bankruptcy section is a comprehensive guide that includes links for forms and additional bankruptcy education.

So, what might these forms include? The following forms are found on the United States Courts website:

B 101		Voluntary Petition for Individuals Filing for Bankruptcy
B 101A		Initial Statement About an Eviction Judgment Against You (individuals)
B 101B		Statement About Payment of an Eviction Judgment Against You
B 103A		Application for Individuals to Pay the Filing Fee in Installments
B 103B		Application to Have the Chapter 7 Filing Fee Waived
B 105		Involuntary Petition Against an Individual
B 106	Declaration	Declaration About an Individual Debtor's Schedules
B 106	Summary	A Summary of Your Assets and Liabilities and Certain Statistical Information (individuals)
B 106A/B		Schedule A/B: Property (individuals)
B 106C		Schedule C: The Property You Claim as Exempt (individuals)
B 106D		Schedule D: Creditors Who Hold Claims Secured By Property (individuals)

© BE Adviser

B 106E/F	Schedule E/F: Creditors Who Have Unsecured Claims (individuals)
B 106G	Schedule G: Executory Contracts and Unexpired Leases (individuals)
B 106H	Schedule H: Your Codebtors (individuals)
B 106I	Schedule I: Your Income (individuals)
B 106J	Schedule J: Your Expenses (individuals) Individual Debtors
B 106J-2	Schedule J-2: Expenses for Separate Household of Debtor 2 (individuals)
B 107	Your Statement of Financial Affairs for Individuals Filing for Bankruptcy
B 108	Statement of Intention for Individuals Filing Under Chapter 7
B 113	Chapter 13 Plan
B 119	Bankruptcy Petition Preparer's Notice, Declaration and Signature
B 121	Your Statement About Your Social Security Numbers
B 122A-1	Chapter 7 Statement of Your Current Monthly Income Means Test Forms

B 122A-1	Supp Statement of Exemption from Presumption of Abuse Under §707(b)(2)
B 122A-2	Chapter 7 Means Test Calculation
B 122C-1	Chapter 13 Statement of Your Current Monthly Income and Calculation of Commitment Period
B 122C-2	Chapter 13 Calculation of Your Disposable Income
B 309A	Notice of Chapter 7 Bankruptcy Case – No Proof of Claim Deadline (For Individuals or Joint Debtors)
B 309B	Notice of Chapter 7 Bankruptcy Case – Proof of Claim Deadline Set (For Individuals or Joint Debtors)
B 309I	Notice of Chapter 13 Bankruptcy Case
B 312	Order and Notice for Hearing on Disclosure Statement
B 313	• Order Approving Disclosure Statement and Fixing Time for Filing • Acceptances or Rejections of Plan, Combined with Notice Thereof
B 314	Ballot for Accepting or Rejecting Plan
B 315	Order Confirming Plan
B 318	Discharge of Debtor in a Chapter 7 Case

© BE Adviser

B 401	Petition for Recognition of Foreign Proceeding
B 410	Proof Of Claim
B 410A	Proof Of Claim, Attachment A
B 410S-1	Proof Of Claim, Supplement 1
B 410S-2	Proof Of Claim, Supplement 2
B 411A	General Power of Attorney
B 411B	Special Power of Attorney
B 416A	Caption
B 416B	Caption (Short Title)
B 416D	Caption for Use in Adversary Proceeding other than for a Complaint Filed by a Debtor
B 420A	Notice of Motion or Objection
B 420B	Notice of Objection to Claim

FILE BANKRUPTCY FOR FREE

B 423	Certification About a Financial Management Course
B 427	Cover Sheet for Reaffirmation Agreement
B 1040	Adversary Proceeding Cover Sheet
B 1130	Motion, Notice and Order for Adequate Protection Payments and Opportunity to Object
B 1310	Exemplification Certificate
B 1320	Application For Search of Bankruptcy Records
B 1330	Claims Register
B 2000	Required Lists, Schedules, Statements, and Fees
B 2010	Notice Required by 11 U.S.C. § 342(b) for Individuals Filing for Bankruptcy
B 2020	Statement of Military Service
B 2030	Disclosure of Compensation of Attorney For Debtor
B 2040	Notice of Need to File Proof of Claim Due to Recovery of Assets

© BE Adviser

B 2050		Notice to Creditors and Other Parties in Interest
B 2060		Certificate of Commencement of Case
B 2070		Certificate of Retention of Debtor in Possesion
B 2100A		Transfer of Claim Other Than For Security
B 2100B		Notice of Transfer of Claim Other Than for Security
B 2300B		Order Confirming Chapter 13 Plan
B 2310B		• Order Fixing Time to Object to Proposed Modification of Confirmed • Chapter 13 Plan
B 2400A		Reaffirmation Documents
B 2400A/B	ALT	Reaffirmation Agreement
B 2400B		Motion For Approval of Reaffirmation Agreement
B 2400C	ALT	Order on Reaffirmation Agreement
B 2400C ALT		Order on Reaffirmation Agreement (Alt.)

B 2500A	Summons in an Adversary Proceeding
B 2500B	Summons and Notice of Pretrial Conference in an Adversary Proceeding
B 2500C	Summons and Notice of Trial in an Adversary Proceeding
B 2500D	Third-Party Summons
B 2500E	Summons to Debtor in Involuntary Case
B 2530	Order For Relief in an Involuntary Case
B 2540	Subpoena For Rule 2004 Examination
B 2550	Subpoena to Appear and Testify at a Hearing or Trial in a Bankruptcy Case (or Adversary Proceeding)
B 2560	Subpoena to Testify at a Deposition in a Bankruptcy Case (or Adversary Proceeding)
B 2570	• Subpoena to Produce Documents, Information, or Objects or to Permit • Inspection of Premises in a Bankruptcy Case (or Adversary Proceeding)
B 2600	Entry of Default
B 2610A	Judgment by Default - Clerk

B 2610B	Judgment by Default - Judge
B 2610C	Judgment in an Adversary Proceeding
B 2620	Notice of Entry of Judgment
B 2630	Bill of Costs
B 2640	Writ of Execution to the United State Marshal
B 2650	Certification of Judgment for Registration in Another District
B 2700	Notice of Filing of Final Report of Trustee
B 2710	<ul><li>Final Decree</li><li>Bankruptcy Forms</li></ul>
B 2800	Disclosure of Compensation of Bankruptcy Petition Preparer
B 2810	Appearance of Child Support Creditor or Representative
B 2830	Chapter 13 Debtor's Certifications Regarding Domestic Support Obligations and Section 522(q)
B 3130S	Order Conditionally Approving Disclosure Statement

B 3150S	Order Approving Disclosure Statement and Confirming Plan
B 3180W	Chapter 13 Discharge
B 3180WH	Chapter 13 Hardship Discharge
B 4100N	Notice of Final Cure Payment
B 4100R	Response to Notice of Final Cure Payment

Overwhelmed? Anyone would be. While this list could easily put you off the notion of filing on your own, keep this in mind: the odds of you needing even half of these forms is very small. If you are qualified for Chapter 7, you won't need any of the Chapter 13 forms. Some of these forms are for creditors, and some are for the courts to use.

This list alone is another good reason to take advantage of websites like CC Advising, UpSolve, and BE Adviser. Their programs are designed to help take the fright out of bankruptcy.

While you won't be able to file with just a handful of forms, most of them are simple, fill in the blank or check the box forms. As stated on UpSolve.org,

> "Having access to the bankruptcy paperwork is only half the battle. You need to figure out what forms you need to file for your own bankruptcy, especially when they have confusing names like "B101" or "B106J." Figuring out what forms you need to fill out will make sure you fill out all the paperwork you need without having to waste time with unnecessary paperwork."

Luckily there are many online resources to help you figure out what forms you need to use for your bankruptcy. Nolo provides a helpful list of bankruptcy forms that most people need to file for a Chapter 7 bankruptcy, starting with form "B101: Voluntary Petition for Individuals Filing for Bankruptcy." There are also more detailed guides to help you deal with all the nuances of specific bankruptcy forms.

Keep in mind that depending on your circumstances you may need to fill out different forms. For instance, if you cannot afford the $335 filing fee for Chapter 7 Bankruptcy then you might want to fill out a form asking for a fee waiver or a form to pay the fee in installments. There are many optional forms like this, so keep that in mind when looking for the right bankruptcy paperwork for your case."

Using the resources discussed in this text will make it easier for you to file for bankruptcy without a costly attorney. Take a look at the forms on the next few pages provided by UpSolve.org. This will give you a sense of how much time filing your petition will take.

Fill in this information to identify your case:

United States Bankruptcy Court for the:

Case number (If known): _____

Chapter you are filing under:
- ☐ Chapter 7
- ☐ Chapter 11
- ☐ Chapter 12
- ☐ Chapter 13

☑ Check if this is an amended filing

Official Form 101

Voluntary Petition for Individuals Filing for Bankruptcy
12/17

The bankruptcy forms use *you* and *Debtor 1* to refer to a debtor filing alone. A married couple may file a bankruptcy case together—called a *joint case*—and in joint cases, these forms use *you* to ask for information from both debtors. For example, if a form asks, "Do you own a car," the answer would be *yes* if either debtor owns a car. When information is needed about the spouses separately, the form uses *Debtor 1* and *Debtor 2* to distinguish between them. In joint cases, one of the spouses must report information as *Debtor 1* and the other as *Debtor 2*. The same person must be *Debtor 1* in all of the forms.

Be as complete and accurate as possible. If two married people are filing together, both are equally responsible for supplying correct information. If more space is needed, attach a separate sheet to this form. On the top of any additional pages, write your name and case number (if known). Answer every question.

Part 1: Identify Yourself

	About Debtor 1:	About Debtor 2 (Spouse Only in a Joint Case):
1. Your full name Write the name that is on your government-issued picture identification (for example, your driver's license or passport). Bring your picture identification to your meeting with the trustee.	First name _____ Middle name _____ Last name _____ Suffix (Sr., Jr., II, III) _____	First name _____ Middle name _____ Last name _____ Suffix (Sr., Jr., II, III) _____
2. All other names you have used in the last 8 years Include your married or maiden names.	First name _____ Middle name _____ Last name _____ First name _____ Middle name _____ Last name _____	First name _____ Middle name _____ Last name _____ First name _____ Middle name _____ Last name _____
3. Only the last 4 digits of your Social Security number or federal Individual Taxpayer Identification number (ITIN)	xxx – xx – ____ ____ ____ ____ OR 9 xx – xx – ____ ____ ____ ____	xxx – xx – ____ ____ ____ ____ OR 9 xx – xx – ____ ____ ____ ____

Fill in this information to identify your case:

Debtor 1 _____
        First Name   Middle Name   Last Name

Debtor 2 _____
(Spouse, if filing) First Name   Middle Name   Last Name

United States Bankruptcy Court for the: _____

Case number _____
(if known)

☐ Check if this is an amended filing

Official Form 106E/F
Schedule E/F: Creditors Who Have Unsecured Claims 12/15

Be as complete and accurate as possible. Use Part 1 for creditors with PRIORITY claims and Part 2 for creditors with NONPRIORITY claims. List the other party to any executory contracts or unexpired leases that could result in a claim. Also list executory contracts on *Schedule A/B: Property* (Official Form 106A/B) and on *Schedule G: Executory Contracts and Unexpired Leases* (Official Form 106G). Do not include any creditors with partially secured claims that are listed in *Schedule D: Creditors Who Have Claims Secured by Property*. If more space is needed, copy the Part you need, fill it out, number the entries in the boxes on the left. Attach the Continuation Page to this page. On the top of any additional pages, write your name and case number (if known).

Part 1: List All of Your PRIORITY Unsecured Claims

1. Do any creditors have priority unsecured claims against you?
   - ☐ No. Go to Part 2.
   - ☐ Yes. ==The most common debts here are tax debts from the past 3 years, child support, and other family support debts.==

2. List all of your priority unsecured claims. If a creditor has more than one priority unsecured claim, list the creditor separately for each claim. For each claim listed, identify what type of claim it is. If a claim has both priority and nonpriority amounts, list that claim here and show both priority and nonpriority amounts. As much as possible, list the claims in alphabetical order according to the creditor's name. If you have more than two priority unsecured claims, fill out the Continuation Page of Part 1. If more than one creditor holds a particular claim, list the other creditors in Part 3.
   (For an explanation of each type of claim, see the instructions for this form in the instruction booklet.)

		Total claim	Priority amount	Nonpriority amount

2.1 _____
Priority Creditor's Name

_____
Number   Street

_____
City   State   ZIP Code

Who incurred the debt? Check one.
- ☐ Debtor 1 only
- ☐ Debtor 2 only
- ☐ Debtor 1 and Debtor 2 only
- ☐ At least one of the debtors and another
- ☐ Check if this claim is for a community debt

Is the claim subject to offset?
- ☐ No
- ☐ Yes

Last 4 digits of account number __ __ __ __

When was the debt incurred? _____

As of the date you file, the claim is: Check all that apply.
- ☐ Contingent
- ☐ Unliquidated
- ☐ Disputed

Type of PRIORITY unsecured claim:
- ☐ Domestic support obligations
- ☐ Taxes and certain other debts you owe the government
- ☐ Claims for death or personal injury while you were intoxicated
- ☐ Other. Specify _____

$_____ $_____ $_____

Type Numbers In Without Commas

2.2 _____
Priority Creditor's Name

_____
Number   Street

_____
City   State   ZIP Code

Who incurred the debt? Check one.
- ☐ Debtor 1 only
- ☐ Debtor 2 only
- ☐ Debtor 1 and Debtor 2 only
- ☐ At least one of the debtors and another
- ☐ Check if this claim is for a community debt

Is the claim subject to offset?
- ☐ No
- ☐ Yes

Last 4 digits of account number __ __ __ __

When was the debt incurred? _____

As of the date you file, the claim is: Check all that apply.
- ☐ Contingent
- ☐ Unliquidated
- ☐ Disputed

Type of PRIORITY unsecured claim:
- ☐ Domestic support obligations
- ☐ Taxes and certain other debts you owe the government
- ☐ Claims for death or personal injury while you were intoxicated
- ☐ Other. Specify _____

$_____ $_____ $_____

Official Form 106E/F   Schedule E/F: Creditors Who Have Unsecured Claims   page 1

Fill in this information to identify your case:

Debtor 1 _____ _____ _____
           First Name   Middle Name   Last Name

Debtor 2 _____ _____ _____
(Spouse, if filing) First Name   Middle Name   Last Name

United States Bankruptcy Court for the: _____

Case number _____
(If known)

Check if this is:
☐ An amended filing
☐ A supplement showing postpetition chapter 13 income as of the following date:
    MM / DD / YYYY

Official Form 106I

Schedule I: Your Income

12/15

Be as complete and accurate as possible. If two married people are filing together (Debtor 1 and Debtor 2), both are equally responsible for supplying correct information. If you are married and not filing jointly, and your spouse is living with you, include information about your spouse. If you are separated and your spouse is not filing with you, do not include information about your spouse. If more space is needed, attach a separate sheet to this form. On the top of any additional pages, write your name and case number (if known). Answer every question.

Part 1: Describe Employment

1. **Fill in your employment information.**

		Debtor 1	Debtor 2 or non-filing spouse
If you have more than one job, attach a separate page with information about additional employers. Include part-time, seasonal, or self-employed work. Occupation may include student or homemaker, if it applies.	Employment status	☐ Employed ☐ Not employed	☐ Employed ☐ Not employed
	Occupation	_____	_____
	Employer's name	_____	_____
	Employer's address	_____ Number Street _____ _____ City State ZIP Code	_____ Number Street _____ _____ City State ZIP Code
	How long employed there?	_____	_____

Part 2: Give Details About Monthly Income

Estimate monthly income as of the date you file this form. If you have nothing to report for any line, write $0 in the space. Include your non-filing spouse unless you are separated.

If you or your non-filing spouse have more than one employer, combine the information for all employers for that person on the lines below. If you need more space, attach a separate sheet to this form.

Confirm that 2 and 3 are correct, looking at the debtor's pay stubs. Remember, you need to double what's on a pay stub if the debtor is paid biweekly. Revise if incorrect.

		For Debtor 1	For Debtor 2 or non-filing spouse
2.	List monthly gross wages, salary, and commissions (before all payroll deductions). If not paid monthly, calculate what the monthly wage would be.	2. $ _____	$ _____
3.	**Estimate and list monthly overtime pay.**	3. +$ _____	+$ _____
4.	**Calculate gross income.** Add line 2 + line 3.	4. $ 0.00	$ _____

Official Form 106I   Schedule I: Your Income   page 1

Fill in this information to identify your case:

Debtor 1 _____
         First Name   Middle Name   Last Name

Debtor 2 _____
(Spouse, if filing) First Name Middle Name   Last Name

United States Bankruptcy Court for the: _____

Case number _____
(If known)

☐ Check if this is an amended filing

Official Form 107
Statement of Financial Affairs for Individuals Filing for Bankruptcy   04/16

Be as complete and accurate as possible. If two married people are filing together, both are equally responsible for supplying correct information. If more space is needed, attach a separate sheet to this form. On the top of any additional pages, write your name and case number (if known). Answer every question.

Part 1: Give Details About Your Marital Status and Where You Lived Before

1. **What is your current marital status?**

   ☐ Married
   ☐ Not married

2. **During the last 3 years, have you lived anywhere other than where you live now?**

   ☐ No
   ☐ Yes. List all of the places you lived in the last 3 years. Do not include where you live now.

Debtor 1:	Dates Debtor 1 lived there	Debtor 2:	Dates Debtor 2 lived there
		☐ Same as Debtor 1	☐ Same as Debtor 1
Number Street	From _____ To _____	Number Street	From _____ To _____
City State ZIP Code		City State ZIP Code	
		☐ Same as Debtor 1	☐ Same as Debtor 1
Number Street	From _____ To _____	Number Street	From _____ To _____
City State ZIP Code		City State ZIP Code	

3. **Within the last 8 years, did you ever live with a spouse or legal equivalent in a community property state or territory?** (*Community property states and territories* include Arizona, California, Idaho, Louisiana, Nevada, New Mexico, Puerto Rico, Texas, Washington, and Wisconsin.)

   ☐ No
   ☐ Yes. Make sure you fill out *Schedule H: Your Codebtors* (Official Form 106H).

Part 2: Explain the Sources of Your Income

Fill in this information to identify your case:

Debtor 1 _____ _____ _____
                First Name   Middle Name   Last Name

Debtor 2 _____ _____ _____
(Spouse, if filing) First Name   Middle Name   Last Name

United States Bankruptcy Court for the: _____

Case number _____
(If known)

Check one box only as directed in this form and in Form 122A-1Supp:

☐ 1. There is no presumption of abuse.

☐ 2. The calculation to determine if a presumption of abuse applies will be made under *Chapter 7 Means Test Calculation* (Official Form 122A–2).

☐ 3. The Means Test does not apply now because of qualified military service but it could apply later.

☐ Check if this is an amended filing

Official Form 122A—1
Chapter 7 Statement of Your Current Monthly Income   12/15

Be as complete and accurate as possible. If two married people are filing together, both are equally responsible for being accurate. If more space is needed, attach a separate sheet to this form. Include the line number to which the additional information applies. On the top of any additional pages, write your name and case number (if known). If you believe that you are exempted from a presumption of abuse because you do not have primarily consumer debts or because of qualifying military service, complete and file *Statement of Exemption from Presumption of Abuse Under § 707(b)(2)* (Official Form 122A-1Supp) with this form.

Part 1: Calculate Your Current Monthly Income

1. **What is your marital and filing status?** Check one only.

   ☐ **Not married.** Fill out Column A, lines 2-11.

   ☐ **Married and your spouse is filing with you.** Fill out both Columns A and B, lines 2-11.

   ==Confirm with debtor that their current monthly income levels below are correct. Debtors sometimes get this incorrect on their own.==

   ☐ **Married and your spouse is NOT filing with you. You and your spouse are:**

      ☐ **Living in the same household and are not legally separated.** Fill out both Columns A and B, lines 2-11.

      ☐ **Living separately or are legally separated.** Fill out Column A, lines 2-11; do not fill out Column B. By checking this box, you declare under penalty of perjury that you and your spouse are legally separated under nonbankruptcy law that applies or that you and your spouse are living apart for reasons that do not include evading the Means Test requirements. 11 U.S.C. § 707(b)(7)(B).

   Fill in the average monthly income that you received from all sources, derived during the 6 full months before you file this bankruptcy case. 11 U.S.C. § 101(10A). For example, if you are filing on September 15, the 6-month period would be March 1 through August 31. If the amount of your monthly income varied during the 6 months, add the income for all 6 months and divide the total by 6. Fill in the result. Do not include any income amount more than once. For example, if both spouses own the same rental property, put the income from that property in one column only. If you have nothing to report for any line, write $0 in the space.

	Column A Debtor 1	Column B Debtor 2 or non-filing spouse
2. **Your gross wages, salary, tips, bonuses, overtime, and commissions** (before all payroll deductions).	$_____	$_____
3. **Alimony and maintenance payments.** Do not include payments from a spouse if Column B is filled in.	$_____	$_____
4. **All amounts from any source which are regularly paid for household expenses of you or your dependents, including child support.** Include regular contributions from an unmarried partner, members of your household, your dependents, parents, and roommates. Include regular contributions from a spouse only if Column B is not filled in. Do not include payments you listed on line 3.	$_____	$_____
5. **Net income from operating a business, profession, or farm** Debtor 1 Debtor 2 Gross receipts (before all deductions) $____ $____ Ordinary and necessary operating expenses − $____ − $____ Net monthly income from a business, profession, or farm $____ $____ Copy here➞	$_____	$_____
6. **Net income from rental and other real property** Debtor 1 Debtor 2 Gross receipts (before all deductions) $____ $____ Ordinary and necessary operating expenses − $____ − $____ Net monthly income from rental or other real property $____ $____ Copy here➞	$_____	$_____
7. **Interest, dividends, and royalties**	$_____	$_____

CHAPTER 4
BEING JUDGMENT PROOF

If you suspect you may be judgment proof, there are specific questions to ask at a free consultation with an attorney to verify your status. According to nolo.com, there are three general conditions that make you judgment proof:

1. do not own any assets such money in a bank account or real estate
2. are not working or have a very low-paying job
3. any other source of income is exempt from seizure by judgment creditors

No Money in a Bank Account

It is not unusual for a creditor will to try to levy against your bank account to satisfy a debt. The creditor requests that the court issue an order to freeze the money in your accounts. Once you file, the levies are lifted and the money sent back to you.

No Real Estate Holdings

When you don't own property, there is no way for a judgment to secure a lien to satisfy a money judgment. If your financial circumstances change and you buy some real estate, the judgment can attach to the property then and you will have to pay the lien before you sell or refinance the home.

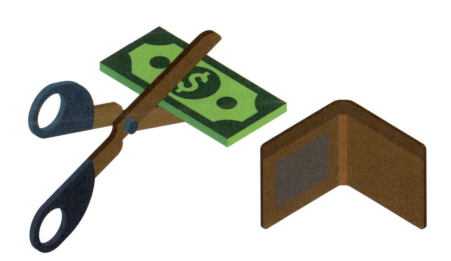

Exempt Income

It is perfectly legal for one or many of your creditors to garnish your income to pay a debt. But, the following sources of income are not within reach of creditors:

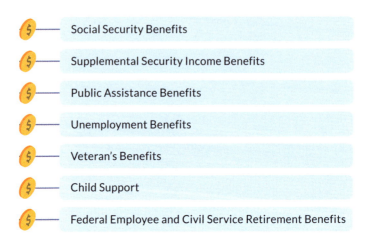

- Social Security Benefits
- Supplemental Security Income Benefits
- Public Assistance Benefits
- Unemployment Benefits
- Veteran's Benefits
- Child Support
- Federal Employee and Civil Service Retirement Benefits

Also, federal law prohibits a judgment creditor from taking your entire paycheck. They can take "25% of your disposable earnings (what's left after mandatory deductions), or the amount by which your wages exceed 30 times the minimum wage, whichever is lower. Some states set a lower percentage limit for how much of your wages can be garnished" (Knapp, 2019).

No Nonexempt Property

While a judgment creditor can try to get your personal property, like a car or jewelry to pay a judgment, they must receive a court order to do so. If a creditor has obtained a judgment against you and tries to enforce it by seizing your cash, or by seizing and selling other real estate, you most likely can keep at least some of that property by using "exemptions."

But, it is not always in the creditor's best interest to levy personal property because it is expensive to seize it, stage it, advertise it, and sell it.

Judgment Proof is not Always a Permanent State

Even if you are currently judgment proof, don't ignore your creditors. Being judgment proof is often a temporary condition and your financial situation could always improve. For instance, you could resume working or inherit assets from an estate.

If you believe you are judgment proof, and a creditor brings a judgment, it is often a good idea to respond to the lawsuit. Judgments last a very long time - and can be renewed. If your financial circumstances could improve in the future, the creditor may be allowed to collect at that time.

If you are not judgment proof, there are certain processes creditors go through to collect on your debt. According to Reiter (2019) on nolo.com, Here are the most common ways judgment creditors collect their judgments from debtors:

Earnings	rate	hours	this period	year to date
Regular	1208.33	86.67	1,208.33	13,510.19
Overtime				177.62
Coml Inc				4,500.00
Hoiliday				334.62
PTO				878.38
St -0/T				13.94
Gross Pay			$1,208.33	19,414.75

Deductions	Stautory		
	Fedaral Income Tax	-19.80	945.55
	Social Security Tax	-74.93	1,203.97
	Medicare Tax	-17.52	281.57
	Other		
	Garnishment	-200.00	
	Manual Adjust	-15.00	
	Std	-17.25	207.00
	Washington L&I	-5.87	

Wage Attachments

First, most judgment creditors go after your paycheck through a wage attachment (also known as wage garnishment). If you are paid regularly, wage attachment is a very effective technique for collection by a judgment creditor. Your employer is required to take a portion of your salary each pay period and sends that money to your creditor.

Federal law allows creditors to take up to either "25% of your net earnings or the amount by which your weekly net earnings exceed 30 times the federal minimum wage, whichever is less. Net earnings are your gross earnings less all legally mandated deductions, such as withheld income taxes and unemployment insurance" (Reiter, 2019).

Higher Wage Attachment Limits for Certain Types of Debts

For certain debts, you will pay more. But, the wage attachment laws and limits described here do not apply to:

> **Child support**
>
> You can lose 50% of your wages to pay support (more if you are behind or don't currently support another dependent). And your child's co-parent usually doesn't have to sue you first (check the law in your state).

> **Income taxes**
>
> It is crucial that you pay what you owe the IRS or the government can take nearly all of your wages. "The weekly garnishment amount (called a levy) is based on the standard income tax deduction, plus the amount for each personal exemption you are entitled to on the income tax form, divided by 52 weeks. If you don't verify the standard deduction and how many dependents you would be entitled to claim on your tax return, the IRS bases the levy on the standard deduction for a married person filing separately, with only one personal deduction—a very low amount. (26 U.S.C. § 6334(d)) (Reiter, 2019).

How a Judgment Creditor Attaches Your Wages

To attach your wages, a judgment creditor gets authorization from the court; this is called a writ. With this authorization, the judgment creditor can direct the local sheriff to seize a portion of your wages. The sheriff notifies your employer of the attachment, and your employer tells you. Unless you object, your employer will send the amount withheld each pay period to the sheriff, the sheriff deducts his or her expenses and sends the balance to the judgment creditor (Reiter, 2019).

> **Objecting to a Wage Attachment**
>
> You can lose 50% of your wages to pay support (more if you are behind or don't currently support another dependent). And your child's co-parent usually doesn't have to sue you first (check the law in your state).

Property Liens

One way judgment creditors can collect is the property lien. In about half the states, a judgment entered against you automatically creates the lien on any real property you own. In all other states, "the creditor must record the judgment with the county, and then the recorded judgment creates a lien on your real property. In a few states, the lien is on your real and personal property. Liens have a lifespan of a few to several years" (Reiter, 2019).

Liens prevent you from selling any real property without paying your creditor. So, if you attempted to sell a car or other high-value property, the court would notify you about the lien. Any profits from the sale would go to the judgment creditor. "Once the judgment creditor has a lien on your property, especially your real property, the creditor can safely anticipate payment. When you sell or refinance your property, title must be cleared—that is, all liens must be removed by paying the lienholder—before the deal can close" (Reiter, 2019).

Executing on the Lien

If the creditor doesn't want to wait for you to sell your property, the creditor can "execute" on the lien. This means the sheriff will seize your property—usually a house—and arrange a public sale from which the creditor is paid out of the proceeds. But if your property is exempt, the creditor cannot do this.

Regardless of the exemption status on your home, many creditors don't like dealing with the hassle and expense of a public sale. "This is especially true if the creditor won't get much money through the sale. Any mortgage holder, government taxing authority, or other creditor who placed a lien on your property before the judgment creditor will be paid first. Then you get any homestead exemption to which you are entitled. Only then does the judgment creditor get his or her share" (Reiter, 2019).

Make Sure the Creditor Followed State Rules When Recording the Lien

A creditor who places a judgment lien on your property must do so legally. Creditors can make mistakes,, which could make the lien unenforceable. "You might have a defense against a creditor's attempt to execute on a lien because the lien is too old or because it was not properly handled. You'll need to consult with an experienced consumer attorney if you suspect that the lien was placed inappropriately or too long ago" (Reiter, 2019).

Property Levies

Another option in collecting for a judgment creditor is a "writ of execution" from the court. They can use this to go after your personal property. The creditor will tell the sheriff or marshal to "levy" it. "Levy" means that the law enforcement officer "takes the property—your baseball card collection, for example—or instructs the holder of the property—your bank, for example—to turn it over to the officer" (Reiter, 2019).

Once secured, the sheriff or marshal sells the property at a public auction and pays off your debt. If a bank account is levied, the money taken from your account is applied to your debt (Reiter, 2019).

Assignment Orders and Contempt Proceedings

An assignment order allows creditors go after property you own that can't be levied, like an anticipated tax refund, the loan value of a life insurance policy, or an annuity policy. Sometimes, the court will issue a judgment that includes a schedule for installments or periodic payments. In a few states, if the judgment doesn't include a repayment schedule, the judgment creditor can ask the judge to make an order requiring periodic payments on a debt. This would be an official court order (Reiter, 2019).

If you don't abide by a court order, the creditor can file for a contempt order. "In a handful of states, if a judge issues an order requiring periodic payments on a debt and you miss any payments, the judge can hold you in contempt. You could be fined, sentenced to community service, or, in theory, at least, the judge could issue a warrant for your arrest and you could be jailed" (Reiter, 2019).

Though this is a blight on your record, arresting a debtor is most likely a very low priority for law enforcement officers, and in most situations, the warrants are never acted on. But the threat of arrest and jail can definitely motivate judgment debtors to make payments ASAP (Reiter, 2019).

[CHAPTER 5]

BE ADVISER – DEBTOR EDUCATION

Filing for bankruptcy after taking the credit counseling course is not the end of the process – far from it. There is a second required bankruptcy course after you file. The website BE Adviser (beadviser.com) provides you with information regarding the rule behind the second course as well as the second course itself. All material presented in this chapter can be found on the beadviser.com website.

Complete Debtor Education Course Online Here
(after you have filed and received a case number):
BEADVISER.COM

DEBTOR EDUCATION

What the Debtor Education Requirement Is Used For

The main purpose of debtor education is to learn about basic concepts related to budgeting, saving, and financial management, to prevent clients who are filing bankruptcy from ever finding themselves in the same situation ever again. Debtor education is required regardless of your pre-existing knowledge or skill level, and regardless of the actual reason you filed bankruptcy.

This requirement is in place so the bankruptcy courts know the person has undergone a basic financial management course, and in effect, has been provided with skills and knowledge that will put them on the road to success after they have gained a fresh start after bankruptcy.

Various Names the Bankruptcy Courses May Be Called

The credit counseling and debtor education requirements go by various names. The courses may be called any of the names on this list.

1ST BANKRUPTCY COURSE (Taken BEFORE filing bankruptcy)

- ▶ Pre-filing Course
- ▶ Credit Counseling

FILE BANKRUPTCY FOR FREE

2ND BANKRUPTCY COURSE (Taken AFTER filing bankruptcy)

- Debtor Education
- Pre-Discharge Course
- Financial Management
- Post-Filing Course

Here's what each of them mean so you can understand the concept of why they're calling the program by these titles; this makes it easier to understand.

1st Bankruptcy Course - Pre-Filing; Credit Counseling Course

If you are taking the pre-filing course (typically required to file bankruptcy), the counselor must analyze your current financial situation, discuss factors that caused that condition, and assist in developing a plan to respond to those problems without incurring negative amortization of debt. The credit counseling provider must be a nonprofit provider and be approved by the United States Trustee program or the Bankruptcy Administrators in Alabama and North Carolina. The credit counseling session takes roughly 60-90 minutes.

2nd Bankruptcy Course - Debtor Education; Financial Management; Post-Filing Course

The purpose of this course is to help instruct you on how to manage your finances and use credit wisely after you have filed for bankruptcy. They want to make sure you can have a fresh start after your bankruptcy is over. The course provider must also be approved by the United States Trustee program, or the Bankruptcy Administrators in Alabama and North Carolina. The debtor education provider takes a minimum of 2 hours or 120 minutes to complete. All providers have the same time requirement.

BE Adviser, LLC is approved in all U.S. States and Territories but not every provider is so it is important to check.

Where Can You Find an Approved Program?

BE Adviser is approved everywhere, their certificates are accepted by all attorneys and in all courts, and most of the top attorneys recommend them, so you are welcome to sign up at beadviser.com. They also have a secure web site and are safe to take the course through.

If you're using a credit counseling organization you must make sure it is a non profit and approved organization. The debtor education course does not have to be provided by a non-profit, but it does have to be approved.

In What Form Can the Bankruptcy Courses Be Taken?

Today, there's good news for busy people with real lives. Depending upon which service you use, the choices are: in person, over the phone; or over the internet

This ensures that regardless of the schedule the person filing has, it's very possible to find a program and course that fit into their everyday life. If the petitioner is having an issue with obtaining credit counseling then they must state why on the petition for bankruptcy. This won't be easy, even in the case of having the life events like eviction, repossession, etc. which may have brought them to bankruptcy in the first place.

In this case, you must explain, not only the reason for the delay in participation but the reasons why, as well as the name of the agency handling your case and contact information. They don't make any concessions for excuses with no plausible explanation or means to verify.

There are exceptions to participation, but the petitioner will have to have section 4 of exhibit D filled out. And in fact, if the petitioner actually qualifies for such an exemption, they'll have to have a proxy to fill out the paperwork. Why? The reason is because the petitioner would have to be mentally or physically incapacitated to the point that they could not participate in the credit counseling requirement at all–not on the internet, by phone or in person.

The only one exception is military personnel on active duty. This also must be proven with government paperwork. So, for the most part, everyone that's filing bankruptcy must participate and within the time allotted.

What to Expect Once The Debtor Education Requirement Is Completed

Once the debtor education is completed, there's things that must be done and the courts are quite precise about how they want it done. When the debtor education requirement is satisfied, the agency you use will provide a certificate of completion.

To generate the certificate, the agency has to use the UST approved certificate generation system or CGS, so it may take a little time. The agency you use will tell you when to expect the certificate and by what means it will be delivered. BE Adviser is committed to issuing these as fast as possible, and many attorneys use them because they are extremely fast and reliable.

How to Obtain The Certificate of Completion

The nice thing about using BE Adviser is that they automatically e-mail the certificate to your attorney, and they make the certificate available in your account with 24/7 access so you can download it at any time.

After you are done with the course, you can download the certificate by logging into your account and downloading it from your profile page. If it says "Pending" it simply means their staff are working on connecting to the UST's certificate generation system so they can create the certificate. It's generally done within minutes during office hours, and on a rolling basis after hours.

Make sure that you provide the correct e-mail for your attorney. Attorneys typically prefer to receive your certificate by e-mail. If you provide an incorrect e-mail address, your certificate may not get delivered. BE Adviser works very hard to correct any mistakes made by their clients. If an e-mail bounces back to them as undeliverable, they will take steps to correct it, but it is better to avoid that problem by providing the correct e-mail in the first place.

Difference Between the Credit Counseling and Debtor Education Courses

The Credit Counseling course is required for all persons filing chapter 7 and chapter 13. However, there is another program that must be taken in these cases called the Debtor Education or Personal Financial Management Course.

This is a bit different but may confuse people because it sounds familiar. In fact, when petitioners find out they have to sit for yet another session, they think there's a mistake or start asking why they have to take the credit counseling over. So, to save a lot of time and energy, we'll explain the difference here.

While the Credit Counseling Course needs to be taken within 180 days prior to filing the actual petition, the Debtor Education Course must be taken, and a certification of completion be awarded after the petition has been filed.

This program can also be called Personal Financial Management or Post-Filing Course, and this is why people think that this is the very program they just got through taking.

As cumbersome as the whole process may be there is a reason for both bankruptcy courses. In fact, it's done separately, not only to satisfy the court but to make sure the petitioner is not confused and understands what's expected of them going forward.

The first Credit Counseling Course takes the form of a session with an approved credit counselor. This deals with the present debt, and the reasons that caused that debt. It is also not presumed that you will necessarily file bankruptcy if you take the credit counseling. Anyone in financial trouble can take it, even if you do not have an attorney. Not everyone who takes credit counseling decides to file bankruptcy, although many do.

Student loans and other types of debt that may not be eligible to be discharged in bankruptcy still have to be managed. And taking the course shows the court that you are capable to use prudent money management skills.

Think about it this way: if you are filing bankruptcy because you have a financial mismanagement issue, then guess what? Best that you get together with a trained credit counseling professional and get it resolved. This is done in several ways but are not limited to these choices. The last thing you want to do is file bankruptcy and get a fresh start, only to end up in a similar situation soon after

What Can You Expect from Each Course?

In this last section, we'll explain what you can expect from each session and offer some tips, so you're prepared fully for the process.

COURSE ONE: THE CREDIT COUNSELING COURSE

Don't worry, this session is completely confidential, so answer their questions honestly. Many clients become embarrassed or guarded when asked about their financial situation, but the counselors are only there to help. They typically will discuss your budget and your current assets and debt, and how you got in debt trouble in the first place. This means the credit counseling professional will take stock of your current debt. For this, you will need to do these things typically but not limited to the below list:

- Make a list of everyone you owe that they have told you, you can't add to the bankruptcy.

- Gather all your statements of credit cards and any bill you can't bankrupt. If you do things online, just print them up.

- Get together a budget on paper as well as you can. You will need your expense report whether you're an individual or a company. They will discuss what you can cut back on and discover where the majority of expense is coming from.

- Get your pay stubs or profit reports together. The income is very important to compare against the current debt that you're left with. Because now, it must be handled.

COURSE TWO: THE DEBTOR EDUCATION COURSE

Now after the first course is done and the current debt is sewn up and you're clear about how to deal with it, the second course begins after the petition for bankruptcy is submitted and accepted. You will receive a case number either from the bankruptcy court or from your attorney. You will need this case number in order to register online for the second course.

The second session is focused on budget planning for after bankruptcy. After the bankruptcy resolves many of your debts, you need to make a plan moving forward to avoid getting into the same situation again. Even if poor financial management was not an issue that caused your bankruptcy (lost your job, had a divorce, or had unexpected medical bills), it helps immensely to plan for the future.

Bankruptcy can last on a public record for no less than 7 years. During this time, typically the petitioner will be credit and financially restrained. You definitely do not want to get into a situation where you are incurring more debt after your bankruptcy is over and threatening your fresh start.

This is the reason why the second course is even more important. These are the things you'll need for that but not limited to the things that are on the list:

- The expense report you brought to the first session
- The clean list of the cutbacks you made within session one
- Most important expenses that you've discussed in session one with the debt counselor.

With these revisions that were made in session one, a new plan is made for exactly what will and will no longer be done with your personal finances. This is meant to establish a healthy attitude and relationship with money. The rest of the course is mostly reading and answering simple questions. There is no way to fail either of the courses, so do not worry about failing or screwing them up. Just be as honest as you can and do the best job you can.

The final tips we can give you to be ahead of the game is this: Be sure to get everything you need gathered and organized regarding your finances. You may receive a list from the people you've chosen to handle your case, but extra research doesn't hurt.

Keep the lines of communication open with the bankruptcy court or your attorney or approved agency and ask as many questions as you feel you need. Follow up with them and submit forms and gather the paperwork they request in a timely manner.

The debtor education process as a whole goes much smoother and efficiently if you are proactive. Any form of financial education stands to be a benefit and the key to a better future where you can enjoy your money with less stress. You will get more out of it if you go into it with a positive attitude.

THE SECOND COURSE

How long does the course take?

The course is required to take a minimum of 120 minutes (2 hours) to complete. The course is timed, and you cannot finish early. Take your time and spend the full two hours on the course material. All debtor education providers have the same time requirement.

You must take the course from an approved provider

The debtor education course must be taken by an approved provider. BE Adviser is approved in all U.S. States and territories, and not every provider is, so you definitely want to check to see whether the provider you choose is approved, either by the US Trustee's office or by the Bankruptcy Administrators (in Alabama and North Carolina).

Same course, different names

It is kind of confusing because the second course goes by various names. 2nd required bankruptcy course, debtor education course, financial management course, post-filing course, pre-discharge course, they all mean the same thing.

How do I sign up for the course?

When signing up for the debtor education course, you need to create a brand new account, which you can do at beadviser.com (click on I NEED an Account). You will also want to have your case number and district handy. Keep in mind, no information from the first course is transferred over. You have to create a brand new account to take the second course.

How can I find my Case Number and District?

Your case number and district are required to sign up for the second bankruptcy course. This information is also printed on your certificate, so you will want to make sure you have the correct information before you register. You will not receive your case number until AFTER your bankruptcy has been filed. If your attorney has not yet filed your paperwork, no case number will be assigned yet. There are 3 main ways to get this information:

- Call VCIS (Voice Case Information System) at: (866) 222-8029 (automated line)
- Ask your attorney
- Ask the bankruptcy court

Will my progress be saved?

If you sign up with BE Adviser, our system automatically saves each page after you submit it. If you are midway through filling out a section and leave, it will not be saved. If you submit the page you are currently on, though, it will be saved. Our system also automatically saves your time spent. You can log out and log back in as many times as you want, and your progress will be saved.

What types of subjects does the course cover?

The BE Adviser debtor education course covers the following topics:

- Budget
- Expense
- Saving
- Saving Money
- Saving Money (continue)
- Using Credit Cards
- Financial Goal Setting
- Financial Record Keeping
- The Difference Between Wants and Needs
- Coping with Unexpected Financial Crisis
- Various Types and Sources of Credit
- Appropriate Uses of Credit and Alternative
- Insurance

Why do I have to fill out a budget?

You may have already filled out a budget for the first credit counseling course, so you may be surprised to find that you also need to fill out a budget for the second debtor education course as well. With the first credit counseling session, a credit counselor uses your budget information to determine whether you have other options other than bankruptcy available to you. The second course is a financial management session, which is more educational. The budget exercise is intended to give you experience planning a budget for use after your bankruptcy.

Is it possible to fail the course?

No, you cannot fail the course. However, you do have to spend the required time (2 hours), and you do need to review the course materials and answer all of the questions correctly.

Will my attorney or bankruptcy court accept your certificate?

Yes, even if you were referred to a different provider, the certificate you receive after completing the BE Adviser debtor education course is accepted everywhere, by all attorneys and by all bankruptcy courts.

HOW DO I MOVE ON?

Once the course is over, you have filed the certification of completion, and gotten your discharge, it is time to start over. While it might be difficult, it will not be impossible to get back on solid ground. The first thing you should do is make sure that whatever debt remains, like child support, student loans, or tax debt, is all taken care of. Get rid of your debt as soon as possible.

Keep current on your bills by paying on time every single month. Never underestimate the power of paying the bills on time. Every single bill and payment you make early or on time helps rebuild your credit. Do yourself a favor and sign up for autopay with whichever creditors you can. This is an automated system that subtracts your payment from your bank account on the same day each month. This way, you are not at risk for forgetting to pay a bill on time. No checks to write or stamps to buy.

Another factor to consider is the order in which you pay bills. Be sure to pay the essential things first- the water bill, the electric, the rent or mortgage, trash and sewer, gas, and car. Then, reserve enough for monthly necessities that vary in price, like groceries and gas. You know you need to eat and you need to fuel your car, but the amount will change slightly and may increase and decrease based on your monthly use.

Finally, divide up most of what is left over for any remaining creditors. Reserve some money every pay period for a savings account, which can pay for emergencies and incidental expenses that could pop up at any time. Many times, large, unexpected expenses can snowball into debt that causes bankruptcy in the first place, so it is wise to prepare for the unexpected.

When you are ready and feel that you are able to handle things like credit cards again, ease in by asking a parent, spouse, or other close friend or family member to add you to one of their credit cards. That way, you have someone to hold you accountable for your spending, and their credit will reflect well on you as you rebuild your score. Again, make sure you are paying your end of things as well in this situation, as it will help to build your credit and help you learn to manage your credit as well.

Next, you may need to purchase a car. In many cases, you will be allowed to keep the car you had as your primary transportation during the bankruptcy process, as long as it is within a financial limit (AKA not a Maserati). But, if your car was repossessed or if you just decided to sell your old wheels to pay off other debts, you may find it difficult getting credit for a new car. But, how you will get to work? If you are not able to pay cash for a car, there is still hope.

It actually is probably better not to pay cash, because this is another opportunity to build your credit, provided you can find someone who is willing to cosign for your loan. A close family member or friend with solid credit is a great resource if you can talk them in to cosigning for your vehicle. They assure the doubtful creditor that they will keep an eye on you and make sure you are paying your car payments in full and on time every month.

If you do not pay on time, your cosigner will be responsible for making up the difference, and they probably would not be very happy with you. When you have a cosigner, it becomes exponentially more important for you to pay your debts on time, because it is no longer just a distant creditor to whom you owe money. Now you also have a personal connection to your creditor, so make sure to be vigilant with payments.

CHAPTER 6
BK FILTER

By now you are probably feeling a bit overwhelmed. Take comfort in the fact that you are not alone. BK Filter (bkfilter.com) is a new website that was designed to create a forum where clients can connect with other clients filing bankruptcy and get advice or ask questions from others who are going through the same process.

The site is up and running, but it is still in the early stages. However, forums like these are a great asset to someone who needs to ask for information or advice and can't afford to pay an attorney to ask. Some attorneys are even members of the forum. You must sign up for a free account to access the forum.

The home page offers you dozens of possible topics to ask questions about:

- 8 Important Bankruptcy Facts
- Bankruptcy is Different in Every State
- Useful Abbreviations
- PACER Information
- Where to get Official Bankruptcy Forms
- Bankruptcy Court fees
- The Civil Cases
- Bankruptcy Appeals
- Bankruptcy Cases
- Credit Counseling and Debtor Education Courses
- The U.S. Trustees
- Securities Investor Protection Act (SIPA)
- How to find a Lawyer
- Discharges in Bankruptcy
- Servicemembers' Civil Relief Act (SCRA)
- Chapter 13 Bankruptcy
- Chapter 12 Bankrupcty
- Chapter 11 Bankruptcy
- 12 Bankruptcy Myths
- Chapter 9 Bankruptcy
- Purpose of Bankruptcy
- Taxes Over View
- Interpersonal Communication
- Warning Signs of Debt Problems
- Money Management
- Types of Loans/Credit
- Budget Development
- Bankruptcy Consumer Education
- The Bankruptcy Process
- 5 Different Types of Bankruptcy
- About Proposals
- Debt Management Program
- Budgeting and Goals
- Short vs Long Term Goals
- Spending Habits
- Merchant "Affinity" Cards
- Types of Garnishments
- Annual Percentage Rate
- Delinquent Debt
- Defining Your Credit Score

- Over the Limit Fees
- Interest Calculations
- How Does Credit Work?
- What Questions Will The Bankruptcy Trustee Ask?
- Exempt vs Non-Exempt Assets
- New Bankruptcy Rules
- Bankruptcy Facts
- How to Avoid Bankruptcy
- Does Bankruptcy Hurt or Help Me?
- Tough Bankruptcy Questions
- Bankruptcy Overview
- More Differences on Chapter 7 and Chapter 13 Bankruptcy
- Collections While Filing for Bankruptcy
- Making a Plan to Buy a Home After Bankruptcy
- How to Pick the Right Attorney For You
- What to Expect at Bankruptcy Meeting of Creditors
- What Bankruptcy Doesn't Clear
- What to Expect While Taking the Pre-filing Course
- Is Bankruptcy Public?
- What to Expect after Filing for Bankruptcy
- Pros and Cons About Filing for Bankruptcy
- 4-Steps to Declare and file for Bankruptcy
- Which Chapter is Right for You?
- New service if you are too broke to go bankrupt
- Helpful Books on Filing Bankruptcy
- Get a Free Credit Report
- What to expect at your 341 Meeting of Creditors
- Bankruptcy Basics
- Free Attorney Finder
- Should I file bankruptcy?
- Documents Your Attorney Needs
- Official Bankruptcy Forms
- Rebuilding Your Credit
- How to Find your Court District

You can post your own questions to the site, and hundreds of other people can respond to the question you posted. The back and forth helps people who are filing really get a handle on where they are in the process, what they need to do next, and where their bankruptcy will eventually take them.

FILE BANKRUPTCY FOR FREE

CHAPTER 7
UPSOLVE

Upsolve.org is a free, legal service for people who want to file Chapter 7 bankruptcy without hiring a lawyer. Users can generate bankruptcy forms and have them reviewed by a lawyer for free. Their online tools ask you questions to help fill in your bankruptcy forms. Their lawyers then review the forms, flagging any inconsistencies or questionable entries.

This is a non-profit organization that was designed by and is run by licensed attorneys. They offer lots of useful information, including bankruptcy guides by state and FAQ's about bankruptcy, creditors, and debt. Many people may wonder how Upsolve manages to be a non-profit organization. The answers lie in the "How It's Free" page with a letter from the CEO, Rohan Pavuluri:

> Dear Community,
>
> Transparency is one of our nonprofit's core values. That's why it's important to us that you know how Upsolve stays free, how we spend our money, and who owns Upsolve.
>
> How is Upsolve free? Upsolve is free for three reasons. First, we receive funding from the government. We're lucky that the government believes that low-income people should receive free access to legal services. The government gives us funding to build and maintain our free tool.
>
> Second, we receive funding from charitable foundations and individuals. Some of these individuals are wealthy people who want to give back. Some of them are Upsolve users who want to pay it forward.
>
> Third, attorneys pay us to market to people who we can't help. When someone who is not low-income takes our screener, we let them know that Upsolve is not right for them, and we ask whether they'd like a free consultation with an attorney. We also let people know they're not the right fit if they're a homeowner, have a pending personal injury case, own over $10,000 in assets, or want to file a joint bankruptcy with their spouse. If the person opts in, we connect them with LegalZoom Local. We always let people who request a private attorney know about the free legal aid options available in their area.

The letter continues, explaining further about the service, who owns it, and how Upsolve responsibly spends its funding. Once you are familiar with Upsolve, you can click on the "How it Works" link.

Their "How It Works" page helps you get started (Upsolve, 2019):

A Step-by-Step Walkthrough for Pro Se Filing

1. Answer a questionnaire about all of your personal finances and upload your pay stubs from the last 60 days, if you were employed (2 hours).

2. Upload your tax returns for the last 2 years, if you filed them (15 mins).

3. Take an online Credit Counseling course, known as Course 1, and get the required certificate. You need this certificate to file your forms. This course costs $14.95 and is offered by another nonprofit that's not Upsolve, but we give you the link that you should use. We show you how to get a fee waiver if you qualify. We automatically get the course certificate and attach it to your bankruptcy forms. (1 hour)

4. Come back to our site and choose a filing date, which tells us when you plan to file your forms. You can file your forms whenever you want, and the Court knows nothing about your filing date. Your filing date just helps you and Upsolve make a plan for when you intend to file.

5. Wait 5 days, as we generate your bankruptcy forms and an in-house Upsolve attorney reviews your forms for you.

6. When we're done reviewing your forms, you'll get an email notification to log back into my.upsolve.org. You'll be able to download and print your forms. You may have to print multiple copies.

7. You need to deliver your forms to the nearest bankruptcy court. You deliver your forms to the Clerk's Office at the bankruptcy court. It's always a good idea to deliver the forms in person if you can, so you guarantee the court accepts them. If you're way too far to deliver your forms in person, you can mail them. You should always call the Clerk's Office ahead of time to find out specific instructions.

Special payment instructions:

- If you're paying the full $335 filing fee at once, make sure to have the cash ready to give to the Clerk's Office all at once.

- If you're paying in installments, make sure to have your first installment payment ready. You should bring at least $100 to file, as some courts don't let you make less than a $100 first installment.

If you're applying for a fee waiver, Upsolve includes the fee waiver at the end of your packet of forms. It's there, we promise. Your fee waiver may be denied, in which case you'll have to pay in installments. Make sure to be alert to see if your fee waiver is denied. Some people get their case dismissed because they weren't aware their fee waiver was denied.

8. Once you file your forms, you will get three important things:

    - The name of your Trustee and their contact information.
    - Direction on what to send to your Trustee. They may request bank statements, your tax returns, your pay stubs, etc. You need to send them all this info ahead of your 341 meeting, or your case will be dismissed.
    - Your 341 Meeting Date

    Your trustee is the court official who oversees your case. You will meet with them about one month after you file your forms. Make sure you save the date of that meeting. If you can't make it, contact your Trustee to reschedule. If you miss this meeting, your case will be dismissed.

9. Mail or email all the documents to your trustee that he requests. These will include the last two years of tax returns. They also likely include your pay stubs, bank statements, car title, etc. Make sure to send your trustee everything they ask for!

10. Take Course 2 online, using our link. This course is a lot like Course 1, and it costs $9.95 but you may be able to get a fee waiver. When you're done, you must save your certificate, print it, and file it with the court. Upsolve doesn't file your Course 2 certificate for you. You should file your certificate with the Clerk's Office the same day as your 341 Meeting, so that you don't forget to do it later. Some people get their case dismissed because they forget to file their Course 2 certificate.

11. Watch the 341 meeting prep video we made for you at my.upsolve.org. This will prepare you for your 5-minute 341 meeting with your trustee.

12. Attend your 341 meeting. Your trustee may say that your case is closed at the end of it, and you won't have to do anything else. You will receive official notice of your debts being erased about two months later in the mail. Your trustee may tell you to make changes to your forms and come back at another date, in which case you should do exactly what they tell you."

Upsolve also has a Learning Center page that offers articles on many bankruptcy topics, including Deciding to File, Chapter 13, After Bankruptcy, Exemptions, Bankruptcy Basics, Debts, Vehicles, Bankruptcy Forms, Filing On My Own, Support Courts, Property, and Wage Garnishment.

To make the site even more appealing, Upsolve offers the testimonies of real clients whose financial lives are back on track thanks to Upsolve. The "Fresh Start Diaries" page is full of success stories from all over the country.

Upsolve is truly a great option for those seeking to file Chapter 7 bankruptcy without an attorney. The resources are valid and up to date, the legal advice is free, and many clients can even benefit from fee waivers during certain stages of the filing process.

If you do use UpSolve, remember to use ccadvising.com for your credit counseling and beadviser.com for your debtor education course. UpSolve may recommend other providers that are more expensive, but they are required to accept certificates from CC Advising and BE Adviser, so you can safely ignore their recommendation for the bankruptcy courses.

CHAPTER 8
BANKRUPTCY COURTS

The website https://www.uscourts.gov/about-federal-courts/federal-courts-public/court-website-links offers information on every district and bankruptcy court in America. To give you a sense of what information is available, let's visit some of those sites (see Appendix B for the complete list).

United States Bankruptcy Court District of Arizona

The home page offers dozens of links for debtors (those filing for bankruptcy) and creditors (those who are owed money).

The Self-Help Center provides a video as well as a comprehensive explanation of how and why one might file for bankruptcy without an attorney. There are additional links within the Self-Help Center that include

- Before You File
- When You File
- After You File
- DeBN (Debtor Electronic Bankruptcy Noticing)
- Creditor FAQs
- Debtor FAQs

United States Bankruptcy Court Southern District of Alabama

As with other court sites, the Southern District of Alabama pages offer links to dozens of articles, places to link to the courts, and an Information tab that includes the following

- Court Locations
- Mobile Courthouse Parking
- Sign Up for Email Notices About Your Case
- Before You File
- After You File
- Discharge in Bankruptcy
- Glossary of Legal Terms
- Chapter 7
- Chapter 11
- Chapter 12
- Chapter 13
- Fees

United States Bankruptcy Court Northern District of Georgia

This website offers many of the same links as the other court sites. The Filing Without an Attorney tab gives you the most useful information:

- Before You File
- After You File
- Discharge
- FAQs
- Fees & Amendments
- Finding a Lawyer
- Glossary of Legal Terms
- Required Forms
- The Reaffirmation Project

United States Bankruptcy Court Eastern District of Missouri

This Missouri court site home page leads with contact information, including phone numbers for the clerk's office (where you file). The Filing Without an Attorney tab includes the following links:

- Bankruptcy Basics
- Chapter 7 Information
- Chapter 13 Information
- Filing Fees
- Filing Requirements
- For Pro Se Filers
- General Bankruptcy Info

United States Bankruptcy Court Northern District of Illinois

This site's home page has links to forms, where to contact the clerk, and frequently used links. The Filing Without an Attorney tab lists the following links:

- Bankruptcy Assistance Desk
- Bankruptcy Basics
- Chapter 7 - Documents Required at Time of Filing (Minimum Filing Requirements)
- Chapter 7 - Additional Documents
- Chapter 13 - Documents Required at Time of Filing (Minimum Filing Requirements)
- Chapter 13 - Additional Documents
- Credit Counseling & Debtor Education Information

- Creditor Matrix Program
- Foreclosure Help
- Glossary Of Bankruptcy Terms
- Guide for Individuals Filing a Bankruptcy without an Attorney
- Illinois Legal Aid
- Notice to Debtors
- Privacy Rules and Policy

United States Bankruptcy Court Middle District of Tennessee

The home page offers the locations of all bankruptcy courts in the state, links for filing an electronic claim, and even job opportunities within the courts. While there is no direct link for filing electronically, there is a tab called Understanding Bankruptcy that includes the following links:

- About the Federal Courts
- Bankruptcy Basics
- Fee Schedule
- Glossary of Legal Terms
- Privacy Policy

If you then click on Bankruptcy Basics, you will get to these links:

- Bankruptcy Basics
- Filing Without an Attorney
- Credit Counseling and Debtor Education
- Trustees and Administrators
- Approved Bankruptcy Notice Providers

From there, you can click on Filing Without an Attorney and get to all the information you need regarding Pro Se filing.

United States Bankruptcy Court Southern District of Indiana

This court site puts its FAQs at the top of the page for ease of access. There is a Filing Without an Attorney tab that gives you the following links:

- Bankruptcy Basics
- Credit Counseling Requirement
- Debtor Electronic Bankruptcy Noticing (DeBN)
- DeBN Frequently Asked Questions (FAQ)
- DeBN Request Form & Docket Event

- ▶ DeBN Requirements
- ▶ Filing Without an Attorney
- ▶ Financial Management Course Requirement
- ▶ Free or Low Cost Legal Help
- ▶ Getting Information About Your Case
- ▶ Legal Advice
- ▶ Legal Services
- ▶ Petition Preparers
- ▶ Pro Se Packet

What's very useful here is the Pro Se Packet, a 22-page .pdf file with a checklist and advice for the filing party.

United States Bankruptcy Court District of Utah

The website for Utah covers the entire state, with related links, resources, and a Filing Without an Attorney tab that takes you to a page with all relevant educational links, process before filing, the pre-filing credit counseling requirement, and more. The page isn't very well-organized and you have to search for what you want. There is no menu of links; rather, they are scattered all over the page.

United States Bankruptcy Court Northern District of Mississippi

This site is very well-organized. The home page offers tabs, including Filing Without an Attorney, and a tab for Links to Helpful Sites:

Links to Helpful Sites

U.S. Trustee

- ▶ Bankruptcy Fraud Hotline(link is external)
- ▶ Region 5 Program(link is external)
- ▶ Credit Counseling & Debtor Education(link is external)
- ▶ Approved Credit Counseling Agencies(link is external)
- ▶ Approved Debtor Education Providers(link is external)

Federal Judiciary

- ▶ PACER Service Center
- ▶ National Creditor Registration Service
- ▶ Federal Courts home page
- ▶ Federal Judicial Center (FJC)(link is external)
- ▶ Fifth Circuit Court of Appeals
- ▶ U. S. District Court - Northern District of Mississippi

Federal Government

- National Archives and Records Administration(link is external)
- United States House of Representatives(link is external)
- United States Senate(link is external)
- The White House(link is external)
- General Services Administration (GSA)(link is external)

Mississippi Sites of Interest

- Mississippi Bankruptcy Conference(link is external)
- Mississippi Supreme Court(link is external)
- Mississippi Secretary of State(link is external)
- State of Mississippi(link is external)
- Mississippi Bar(link is external)
- Mississippi Bar-MS Volunteer Lawyers Project(link is external)

Legal Assistance

- American Bar Association - Consumer's Guide to Legal Help on the Internet

The Filing Without an Attorney tab includes an overview of the process along with the following links:

- Bankruptcy
- Bankruptcy Basics
- Filing Without an Attorney
- Credit Counseling and Debtor Education
- Trustees and Administrators
- Approved Bankruptcy Notice Providers

United States Bankruptcy Court Western District of Kentucky

Like most other court sites, the home page has tabs and links to the courts themselves, information for attorneys, and contact information. The site includes a page on Pro Se resources that includes the following:

If you do not have an attorney, and you are filing or involved in a bankruptcy case in the U.S. Bankruptcy Court for the Western District of Kentucky, you may get information about the overall bankruptcy process and general filing requirements by viewing the contents of this website and/or from the Court's Guide to Filing Bankruptcy without an Attorney. The staff of the U.S. Bankruptcy Court Clerk's office provides a variety of services; however, they are not permitted to assist with the preparation of the voluntary

petition, schedules, or other documents, nor can they provide legal advice.
While the information presented below is accurate as of the date of publication, it should not be cited or relied upon as legal authority. It is highly recommended that legal advice be obtained from a bankruptcy attorney or legal association. For filing requirements, please refer to the United States Bankruptcy Code (Title 11, United States Code), the Federal Rules of Bankruptcy Procedure(Bankruptcy Rules), the Local Rules for the United States Bankruptcy Court for the Western District of Kentucky and at the U.S. Courts website at www.uscourts.gov/bankruptcycourts/prose.html.

The above listed sites were chosen because those were the top states and regions in terms of number of bankruptcies filed per year in 2016 (that is the most current data available). If you are searching for your district or state website, see Appendix B.

CONCLUSION

Filing for bankruptcy is a scary thing. If you have gotten to that point, you are probably swimming in debt, have creditors calling day and night, and have run out of options to pay off your debt. But, bankruptcy doesn't have to be scary or expensive. The resources available today, thanks to the internet, make it possible for you to find competent bankruptcy attorneys in your area, find free legal aid if you qualify, or, as a last resort, file bankruptcy on your own.

If you can find the money to file bankruptcy, it is always preferable to hire competent counsel to represent you. However, if you're reading this book, you probably are looking for ways to avoid that cost, and that's why we provide you with the tools and resources for you to thoroughly evaluate any and all other options.

Start by taking the credit counseling course (**CC Advising**, **ccadvising.com**). They charge a small fee for the course, but you can request a waiver of the fee if necessary. Taking the credit counseling course will help you determine if bankruptcy is a truly necessary step, or if there are alternatives you can choose to pay off your debts. If you sign up Pro Se (meaning you do not have an attorney yet), they will even show you attorneys in your area who may be able to help.

If you still need to file, check your eligibility for Chapter 7 first. It is the most comprehensive way to wipe out debt, and while we always recommend hiring an attorney, it is possible to do it on your own. If you don't qualify for Chapter 7, Chapter 13 will be your other option (debt reorganization), but don't get sucked into a Fee-Only Bankruptcy Plan or you will be paying for years to not only get rid of debt, but also to pay the attorney's fee.

While there are multiple places to find your bankruptcy forms online, its best to get them for free. All forms are available through the United States Courts website, but make sure you get them for your current location (see Appendix B).

Even though you may be ready to file, there is a possibility that you are judgment proof – meaning that creditors cannot seize your property, cash, or other assets. However, don't make this assumption. Carefully research what it means to be judgment proof before heading down that path (Chapter 4).

After filing (and after you have received your case number), you will need to complete your Debtor Education course with **BE Adviser**, **beadviser.com**, as well. This will help you re-focus your finances, reinforce the importance of following a budget, and give you advice on how to properly save your money.

If you are ready to tear your hair out by now, visit **BK Filter, bkfilter.com,** and talk with others who are in your situation. The forum has lots of detailed information about the bankruptcy process and hundreds of posts from real life people going through bankruptcy just like you.

Of all the places we've examined, UpSolve is the one-stop shop that gives you all you need in terms of filling out forms, filing for bankruptcy, and reading about the successes of their clients. Just make sure you use CC Advising for your credit counseling and BE Adviser for your debtor education course. Upsolve may try to direct you to different providers, but rest assured they are required to accept certificates from CC Advising and BE Adviser.

Do not be misled by scam companies who are offering software to let you file bankruptcy on your own. Many of these companies are just repackaging the same forms you can get online for free, and then charging you for them. Also stay away from non-attorneys or so called "petition preparers". These may be paralegals or other non-attorneys who offer to fill out the forms for you, but they do not have the required training or experience, and when you submit the forms to the court, you will be on the hook if they have made mistakes.

Finally, you can find detailed information about the bankruptcy courts by visiting the United States Courts website. We reviewed several state sites to give you an example of what types of information are available.

No matter what your current situation may be, don't act rashly. Don't run out and retain an attorney without first doing some valuable research and finding out what you can on your own. Being your own advocate is the best way to ensure that your case is handled appropriately and in your best interest.

The ideal situation is that after taking the required credit counseling with **CC Advising, ccadvising.com,** you save up enough money to hire a bankruptcy attorney who is well-respected (preferably a NACBA member). After that, if you still do not have the money to file, try getting ahold of some legal aid organizations in your area. If that does not work, see if Upsolve is available in your area. The riskiest option is to file on your own. It is possible if you have a very simple Chapter 7 case, but you should buy the NOLO book, *How to File for Chapter 7 Bankruptcy*, and read it cover to cover before you even try attempting this, it is not recommended.

Take the **BE Adviser, beadviser.com** course after your case has been filed and after you have received a case number from your attorney or from the bankruptcy court. This is the second required debtor education course that is necessary to take in bankruptcy.

Lastly, attached to this guide are two wonderful Appendices which are worth their weight in gold. Appendix A is a State by State list of Legal Aid Organizations. If you are low income or otherwise qualify, they may be able to assist you in filing bankruptcy for free. At the least, it will not hurt to call and ask. Even if you're trying to file bankruptcy for free, having legal counsel is always preferred to going through the process alone.

Remember, most bankruptcy attorneys will provide an initial consultation free of charge, so it never hurts to visit a few of them (even if you don't think you can afford going further) to see what options they give you.

Appendix B has the links to all of the bankruptcy court web sites, where you can find valuable information relevant to the district you will be filing bankruptcy in.

If you get stuck at all, feel free to sign up for **BK Filter, bkfilter.com** and communicate with other individuals who are going through the same process.

REFERENCES

American Bankruptcy Institute. (2019). The Changing Profile of Chapter 7 Filers Detailed in September ABI Journal Article. Retrieved from
https://abi.org/newsroom/press-releases/the-changing-profile-of-chapter-7-filers-detailed-in-september-abi-journal

BE Adviser. (2019). Debtor Education Requirement. Retrieved from
https://beadviser.com/articles/debtor-education-requirement

BE Adviser. (2019). Ultimate Guide to Debtor Education, The Second Bankruptcy Course. Retrieved from
https://beadviser.com/articles/ultimate-guide-to-debtor-education-the-second-bankruptcy-course

Bulkat, B. (2019). What Are My Options If I Can't Afford a Bankruptcy Attorney? Retrieved from
https://www.alllaw.com/articles/nolo/bankruptcy/bankruptcy-options-cant-afford-attorney.html

CC Advising. (2018). Pre-Bankruptcy Credit Counseling Requirement. Retrieved from
https://ccadvising.com/articles/pre-bankruptcy-credit-counseling-requirement

CC Advising. (2018). Ultimate Guide to Credit Counseling. Retrieved from
https://ccadvising.com/articles/ultimate-guide-to-credit-counseling-the-first-bankruptcy-course

Justia Lawyers. (2019). Bankruptcy Lawyers. Retrieved from
https://www.justia.com/lawyers/bankruptcy

Knapp, J. (2019). What Does Judgment Proof Mean? Retrieved from
https://www.nolo.com/legal-encyclopedia/what-does-judgment-proof-mean.html

National Association of Consumer Bankruptcy Attorneys. (2017). Find an Attorney. Retrieved from
https://www.nacba.org/find-an-attorney/

Nolo.org. (2019). Which Type of Bankruptcy is right for Me? The Bankruptcy Site. Retrieved from
https://www.thebankruptcysite.org/resources/bankruptcy/bankruptcy-planning/which-is-right-who-file.htm

O'Neill, C. (2019). What are the Differences Between Chapter 7 and Chapter 13 Bankruptcy? Retrieved from https://www.nolo.com/legal-encyclopedia/what-is-the-difference-between-chapter-7-chapter-13-bankrutpcy.html

Reiter, M. (2019). How Creditors Enforce Judgments. Retrieved from https://www.nolo.com/legal-encyclopedia/how-creditors-enforce-judgments.html

United States Courts. (2018). District and Bankruptcy Courts. Retrieved from https://www.uscourts.gov/about-federal-courts/federal-courts-public/court-website-links

United States Courts. (2018). Just the Facts: Consumer Bankruptcy Filings, 2006-2017. Retrieved from https://www.uscourts.gov/news/2018/03/07/just-facts-consumer-bankruptcy-filings-2006-2017

Upsolve. (2019). How Upsolve Works. Retrieved from https://upsolve.org/how-we-work/

APPENDIX A

State by State list of Legal Aid Organizations
(Retrieved from https://www.justia.com/lawyers/bankruptcy)

Alabama

Alabama State Bar Volunteer Lawyers Program
(334) 269-1515
415 Dexter Ave
Montgomery, AL 36104

Bankruptcy, Consumer, Divorce and Education
Legal Services Of Metro Birmingham, Inc PAI & VLP Program
(800) 819-7685
1820 Seventh Avenue North
Birmingham, AL 35203

Bankruptcy, Consumer, Divorce and Education
Legal Services Corporation of Alabama, Inc. Tuscaloosa Regional Office
(205) 758-7503
1351 McFarland Blvd E 11th Floor
Tuscaloosa, AL 35404

Bankruptcy, Civil Rights, Consumer and Criminal
LRIS Of Madison County, Inc Lawyer Referral & Information Service
(205) 539-2275
PO Box 2913
Huntsville, AL 35804
Bankruptcy, Civil Rights, Consumer and Criminal

Alaska

Alaska Department of Law, Consumer Protection
1031 W. 4th Avenue
Anchorage, AK 99501
http://www.law.state.ak.us/department/civil/consumer/cpindex.html

Alaska Institute for Justice
431 West 7th Ave. Suite 208
Anchorage, AK 99501
907-279-2457
http://www.akijp.org/

Alaska Legal Services - Anchorage
1016 W. 6th Avenue Ste. 200
Anchorage, AK 99501
907-272-9431
https://www.alsc-law.org/

Alaska Legal Services - Bethel
PO Box 248 BNC building #213
Bethel, AK 99559
907-543-2237
https://www.alsc-law.org/

Alaska Legal Services - Bristol Bay Office
1500 Kanakanak Road/PO Box 176
Dillingham, AK 99576
907-842-1452
https://www.alsc-law.org/

Alaska Legal Services - Fairbanks
100 Cushman St. 500
Fairbanks, AK 99701
907-452-5181
https://www.alsc-law.org/

Alaska Legal Services - Juneau
8800 Glacier Highway Suite 228
Juneau, AK 99801
907-586-6425
https://www.alsc-law.org/

Alaska Legal Services - Kenai
PO Box 2463 110 N. Willow Street
Kenai, AK 99611
907-395-0352
https://www.alsc-law.org/

Alaska Legal Services - Ketchikan
2417 Tongass Ave. Unit 202 B
Ketchikan, AK 99901
907-225-6420
https://www.alsc-law.org/

Alaska Legal Services - Kotzebue
PO Box 526
Kotzebue, AK 99752
907-442-7737
https://www.alsc-law.org/

Alaska Legal Services - Mat Su
634 S. Bailey St., Ste. 102
Palmer, AK 99645
907-746-4636
https://www.alsc-law.org/

Alaska Legal Services- Nome
PO Box 1429 110 Front Street, Suite 201
Nome, AK 99762
907-443-2230
https://www.alsc-law.org/

Alaska Legal Services - Utqiagvik (Barrow)
PO Box 1651 1264 Agvik Street, Space 7
Barrow, AK 99723
907-855-8998
https://www.alsc-law.org/

Alaska Native Justice Center
3600 San Jeronimo Drive, Ste. 264
Anchorage, AK 99508
907-793-3550
http://www.anjc.org

Arizona

Maricopa County Volunteer Lawyers Program
(602) 506-7948
PO Box 21538
Phoenix, AZ 85003
Bankruptcy, Civil Rights, Consumer and Criminal

Upsolve
305 S. 2nd Ave.
Phoenix, AZ 85003
Bankruptcy

Southern Arizona Legal Aid, Inc. - Pinal County Office
(520) 316-8076
1729 North Trekell Rd
Casa Grande, AZ 85122
Bankruptcy, Consumer, Criminal and Divorce

Southern Arizona Legal Aid, Inc. - Gila, Navajo & Apache Counties Office White Mountain Legal Ai
(928) 537-8383
5658 Highway 260, Suite 15
Lakeside, AZ 85929
Bankruptcy, Consumer, Criminal and Divorce

Parker Senior Center Legal Clinic
(520) 669-9514
1115 N 12th St
Parker, AZ 85344
Bankruptcy, Civil Rights, Consumer and Criminal

Pima County Volunteer Lawyers Program
(520) 623-9461
2343 Broadway Blvd
Tucson, AZ 85719
Bankruptcy, Civil Rights, Consumer and Criminal

Southern Arizona Legal Aid, Inc. Douglas, Cochise County Office
(520) 364-7973
1065 F Ave
Douglas, AZ 85607
Bankruptcy, Consumer, Criminal and Divorce

Arkansas

Central Arkansas Legal Services
(501) 376-3423
1300 W 6th St
Little Rock, AR 72201
Bankruptcy, Civil Rights, Consumer and Criminal

Arkansas Volunteer Lawyers for the Elderly
(800) 234-3544
2020 W 3rd St, Ste 620
Little Rock, AR 72205
Bankruptcy, Consumer, Divorce and Elder

Legal Services of Northeast Arkansas
(870) 523-9892
202 Walnut St
Newport, AR 72112
Bankruptcy, Consumer, Criminal and Divorce

Center for Arkansas Legal Services, Inc. River Valley Volunteer Attorney Project
(800) 364-1134
PO Box 8105
Fort Smith, AR 72901
Bankruptcy, Consumer, Criminal and Divorce

California

Legal Services for Seniors
(831) 899-0492
915 Hilby Avenue,
Seaside, CA 93955
Bankruptcy, Consumer, Elder and Estate Planning

AIDS Legal Services
(408) 293-3135
111 W Saint John St, Ste 315
San Jose, CA 95113
Bankruptcy, Civil Rights, Consumer and Divorce

California Lawyers for the Arts
(888) 775-8995
12304 Santa Monica Blvd., Ste. 304
Los Angeles, CA 90025
Bankruptcy, Business, Civil Rights and Consumer

Voluntary Legal Services Program of Northern California, Inc.
(916) 551-2102
501 12th Street
Sacramento, CA 95814
Bankruptcy, Consumer, Criminal and Elder

San Luis Obispo Legal Alternatives Corporation
(805) 543-5140
3437 Empresa Drive
San Luis Obispo, CA 93401
Bankruptcy, Consumer, Criminal and Divorce

Nevada County Lawyer Referral Service
(530) 888-1836
120 N. Auburn St.
Grass Valley, CA 95945
Bankruptcy, Consumer, Divorce and Elder

Bar Association of San Francisco Volunteer Legal Services Program
(415) 982-1600
301 Battery Street
San Francisco, CA 94111
Bankruptcy, Civil Rights, Consumer and Criminal

AIDS Legal Referral Panel of the San Francisco Bay Area
(415) 701-1100
1663 Mission St.
San Francisco, CA 94103
Bankruptcy, Civil Rights, Consumer and Divorce

Legal Aid of North Bay Private Attorney Involvement Program
1227 Coombs St
Napa, CA 94559
Bankruptcy, Civil Rights, Consumer and Criminal

Legal Aid of Napa Valley
(707) 255-4933
1277 Coombs Street
Napa, CA 94559
Bankruptcy, Consumer, Divorce and Elder

North Bay Legal Aid
(415) 492-0230
30 N San Pedro Rd
San Rafael, CA 94903
Bankruptcy, Civil Rights, Consumer and Criminal

AIDS Care Legal Clinic
(805) 643-0446
632 E Thompson Blvd
Ventura, CA 93001
Bankruptcy, Civil Rights, Consumer and Estate Planning

Sonoma County Legal Services Foundation
(707) 546-2924
1212 4th St, Ste I
Santa Rosa, CA 95404
Bankruptcy, Collections, Criminal and Employment

Conejo Free Clinic Legal Services
(805) 497-3575
80 E Hillcrest Dr
Thousand Oaks, CA 91360
Bankruptcy, Civil Rights, Consumer and Criminal

Los Angeles Free Clinic
(323) 653-8622
8405 Beverly Blvd
Los Angeles, CA 90048
Bankruptcy, Divorce, Family and Immigration

Public Counsel
(213) 385-2977
601 S Ardmore Ave
Los Angeles, CA 90005
Bankruptcy, Civil Rights, Consumer and Family

AIDS Project Los Angeles, HIV & AIDS Legal Services Project
(213) 201-1600
611 S. Kingsley Dr.
Los Angeles, CA 90005
Bankruptcy, Civil Rights, Employment and Estate Planning

Bet Tzedek Legal Services
(323) 939-0506
3250 Wilshire Blvd., 13th Floor
Los Angeles, CA 90010
Bankruptcy, Civil Rights, Consumer and Elder

Legal Aid Foundation of Los Angeles
(213) 640-3881
1550 West 8th Street
Los Angeles, CA 90017
Bankruptcy, Consumer, Criminal and Domestic Violence

San Gabriel Valley LRS
(626) 966-5530
1175 E Garvey Ave, Ste 105
Covina, CA 91724
Bankruptcy, Consumer, Criminal and Divorce

Legal Services Program for Pasadena and San Gabriel-Pomona Valley
(909) 622-7455
243 W Mission Blvd, Ste 303
Pomona, CA 91766
Bankruptcy, Criminal, Divorce and Family

Legal Aid Society of Orange County
(310) 638-6194
725 W. Rosecrans
Compton, CA 90222
Bankruptcy, Civil Rights, Consumer and Divorce

Legal Aid Society of San Diego
(877) 534-2454
250 E. Main Street
El Cajon, CA 92020
Bankruptcy, Civil Rights, Consumer and Criminal

San Diego Volunteer Lawyer Program
(619) 235-5656
707 Broadway
San Diego, CA 92101
Bankruptcy, Business, Civil Rights and Criminal

Colorado

Northwest Colorado Legal Services
(970) 641-3023
P.O. Box 963
Gunnison, CO 81230
Bankruptcy, Consumer, Criminal and Divorce

Metro Volunteer Lawyers
(303) 860-1115
1905 Sherman St, Ste 400
Denver, CO 80203
Bankruptcy, Civil Rights, Consumer and Divorce

Boulder County Legal Services (BCLS)
(303) 449-7575
315 W South Boulder Rd #205
Louisville, CO 80027
Bankruptcy, Civil Rights, Consumer and Divorce

Garfield Legal Services, Inc.
(970) 945-8858
109 8th St, Ste 304
Glenwood Springs, CO 81601
Bankruptcy, Consumer, Criminal and Divorce

Uncompahgre Volunteer Legal Aid
(970) 249-7202
300 N Cascade Ave
Montrose, CO 81401
Bankruptcy, Consumer, Criminal and Divorce

Delta County Bar Association Pro Bono Program
(970) 243-7940
Delta County Courthouse
Delta, CO 81416
Bankruptcy, Consumer, Criminal and Divorce

Pro Bono Project of Mesa County
(970) 424-5748
619 Main Street
Grand Junction, CO 81501
Bankruptcy, Consumer, Divorce and Elder

Northeast Colorado Legal Services
(970) 522-6391
Room 22 Walker Hall
Sterling, CO 80751
Bankruptcy, Consumer, Criminal and Divorce

Southwest Bar Volunteer Legal Aid, Inc.
(970) 247-0266
1474 Main Ave, Ste 108
Durango, CO 81301
Bankruptcy, Consumer, Criminal and Divorce

Connecticut
Statewide Legal Services of Connecticut, Inc.
(860) 344-8096
Ext. 30
425 Main St
Middletown, CT 06457
Bankruptcy, Civil Rights, Consumer and Criminal

Upsolve
1290 Silas Deane Hwy
Wethersfield, CT 06109
Bankruptcy

AIDS Legal Network for Connecticut (ALN)
80 Jefferson St
Hartford, CT 06106
Bankruptcy, Civil Rights, Consumer and Divorce

Greater Hartford Legal Assistance, Inc.
(860) 541-5000
999 Asylum Avenue, 3rd Floor
Hartford, CT 06105
Bankruptcy, Consumer, Divorce and Estate Planning

Delaware

Delaware Volunteer Legal Services, Inc.
(302) 478-8680
4601 Concord Pike
Wilmington, DE 19803
Bankruptcy, Civil Rights, Consumer and Criminal

Florida

Gulfcoast Legal Services
(727) 443-0657
2189 Cleveland Street, Building G, Suite 210
Clearwater, FL 33765
Bankruptcy, Civil Rights, Consumer and Divorce

Community Law Program
(727) 582-7402
501 1st Avenue North
St. Petersburg, FL 33701
Bankruptcy, Divorce, Family and Real Estate

Community Law Program
(727) 582-7402
501 First Avenue N, Room 519
Saint Petersburg, FL 33701
Bankruptcy, Consumer, Divorce and Estate Planning

Legal Aid of Manasota, Inc.
(941) 366-0038
1900 Main St., Ste. 302
Sarasota, FL 34236
Bankruptcy, Civil Rights, Consumer and Divorce

Bay Area Legal Services
(813) 232-1343
1302 N. 19th Street, Suite 400
Tampa, FL 33605
Bankruptcy, Business, Civil Rights and Consumer

Volunteer Involvement Project, Affordable Legal Services
PO Box 24688
Lakeland, FL 33802
Bankruptcy, Civil Rights, Consumer and Criminal

Upsolve
122 E Colonial Dr # 200
Orlando, FL 32801
Bankruptcy

Three Rivers Legal Services, Inc.
(904) 394-7450
3225 University Blvd South
Jacksonville, FL 32216
Bankruptcy, Civil Rights, Consumer and Criminal

Legal Advocacy Center of Central Florida
(407) 708-1020
315 Magnolia Ave
Sanford, FL 32771
Bankruptcy, Consumer and Real Estate

Legal Services of North Florida Private Bar Involvement Program
(850) 769-3581
211 E. 11th St.
Panama City , FL 32401
Bankruptcy, Civil Rights, Consumer and Criminal

Legal Aid Service of Broward County, Inc.
(954) 765-8957
Ext. 27
491 North State Road 7
Plantation, FL 33317
Bankruptcy, Civil Rights, Consumer and Divorce

Dade County Put Something Back Pro Bono Project
123 NW 1st Ave
Miami, FL 33128
Bankruptcy, Civil Rights, Consumer and Criminal

Legal Aid Society of Dade County Bar Association
(305) 579-5733
123 NW 1st Ave.
Miami, FL 33128
Bankruptcy, Civil Rights, Consumer and Divorce

© BE Adviser

Northwest Florida Legal Services, Inc.
(850) 432-3999
701 South J Street
Pensacola, FL 32502
Bankruptcy, Civil Rights, Consumer and Criminal

Georgia

Georgia Legal Services Program, Inc.
(706) 227-5362
525 S. Milledge Avenue
Athens, GA 30603
Bankruptcy, Civil Rights, Consumer and Divorce

DeKalb Volunteer Lawyers Foundation
(404) 373-0865
315 W. Ponce De Leon Ave 561
Decatur, GA 30030
Bankruptcy, Consumer, Criminal and Divorce

Gwinnett County Pro Bono Project
(678) 376-4545
324 W. Pike Street Suite 200
Lawrenceville, GA 30046
Bankruptcy, Consumer, Criminal and Divorce

Clayton County Pro Bono Project
(404) 524-5811
54 Ellis Street, NE
Atlanta, GA 30303
Bankruptcy, Civil Rights, Consumer and Criminal

Atlanta Volunteer Lawyers Foundation
(404) 521-0790
235 Peachtree Street NW
Atlanta, GA 30303
Bankruptcy and Landlord Tenant

Hawaii

Volunteer Legal Services of Hawaii
(808) 528-7046
545 Queen St, Ste 100
Honolulu, HI 96813
Bankruptcy, Consumer, Criminal and Divorce

FILE BANKRUPTCY FOR FREE

Idaho

Boise
1447 S Tyrell Lane
Boise, ID 83706
208-345-0106
Telecommunication Relay Service (TRS), dial 711

Caldwell
212 12th Ave Road
Nampa, ID 83686
208-454-2591
Telecommunication Relay Service (TRS), dial 711

Coeur d'Alene
610 W. Hubbard Ave.
Suite 219
Coeur d'Alene, ID 83814
208-667-9559
Telecommunication Relay Service (TRS), dial 711

Idaho Falls
482 Constitution Way
Ste. 101
Idaho Falls, ID 83402
208-524-3660
Telecommunication Relay Service (TRS), dial 711

Lewiston
2230 3rd Ave North
Lewiston, ID 83501
208-743-1556
Telecommunication Relay Service (TRS), dial 711

Pocatello
150 S. Arthur
No. 203
Pocatello, ID 83204
208-233-0079
Telecommunication Relay Service (TRS), dial 711

Twin Falls
475 Polk
Suite 4
Twin Falls, ID 83301
208-734-7024
Telecommunication Relay Service (TRS), dial 711

Upsolve
1447 S Tyrell Lane
Boise, ID 83706
Bankruptcy

© BE Adviser

Illinois

Prairie State Legal Services, Inc.
(309) 827-5021
201 W. Olive Street
Bloomington, IL 61701
Bankruptcy, Civil Rights, Consumer and Criminal

Land of Lincoln Legal Assistance Foundation, Inc.
(618) 398-0958
8787 State #101
East St. Louis, IL 62203
Bankruptcy, Consumer, Divorce and Education

DuPage Bar Legal Aid Service
(630) 653-6212
126 S County Farm Rd
Wheaton, IL 60187
Bankruptcy, Criminal, Divorce and Estate Planning

Chicago Legal Clinic Pro Bono Program
(773) 731-1762
2938 E 91st St
Chicago, IL 60617
Bankruptcy, Civil Rights, Consumer and Divorce

Legal Assistance Foundation of Metropolitan Chicago
(312) 341-1070
120 S. LaSalle Ste 900
Chicago, IL 60603
Bankruptcy, Civil Rights, Consumer and Criminal

Chicago Volunteer Legal Services Foundation
(312) 332-1624
33 North Dearborn Street,
Chicago, IL 60602
Bankruptcy, Civil Rights, Consumer and Criminal

Legal Clinic for the Disabled, Inc.
(312) 908-4463
710 N Lake Shore Dr
Chicago, IL 60611
Bankruptcy, Civil Rights, Education and Employment

Lake County Bar Foundation Volunteer Lawyers Program
(847) 662-6925
415 Washington St
Waukegan, IL 60085
Bankruptcy, Civil Rights, Consumer and Divorce

Indiana
Regional Offices

Indiana Legal Services - Bloomington
214 South College Ave.
Second Floor
Bloomington, IN 47404
Office - 812-339-7668
The Bloomington office serves Bartholomew, Brown, Clay, Greene, Jackson, Lawrence, Monroe, Morgan, Orange, Owen, Parke, Putnam, Sullivan, and Vigo counties.

Indiana Legal Services - Columbus
Area XI Council on Aging
1531 13th Street, Suite G
Columbus, IN 47201-1302
Phone: (812) 372-6918
Toll-Free: (866) 644-6407
The Columbus office handles Senior Law issues for Bartholomew, Brown, Decatur, Jackson, and Jennings counties.

Indiana Legal Services - Evansville
111 S.E. Third Street
Suite 205
Evansville, IN 47708
Phone: (812) 426-1295
Toll-Free: (800) 852-3477
Intake: (844) 243-8570 (toll free)
The Evansville office serves Daviess, Dubois, Gibson, Knox, Martin, Perry, Pike, Posey, Spencer, Vanderburgh, and Warrick counties.

Indiana Legal Services - Ft. Wayne
919 S. Harrison St.
Suite 200
Fort Wayne, IN 46802
Phone: (260) 424-9155
Toll-Free: (888) 442-8600
The Fort Wayne office serves Adams, Allen, Blackford, Dekalb, Grant, Huntington, Jay, Steuben, Wells, and Whitley counties.

Indiana Legal Services - Indianapolis
151 N Delaware St
Suite 1800
Indianapolis, IN 46204
Office - (317) 631-9410
Intake - (844) 243-8570 (toll free)
The Indianapolis office serves Boone, Decatur, Delaware, Fayette, Franklin, Hamilton, Hancock, Hendricks, Henry, Johnson, Madison, Marion, Randolph, Rush, Shelby, Union, and Wayne counties.

Indiana Legal Services - Lafayette
8 N 3rd Street
Suite 102
Lafayette, IN 47901
Office: (765) 423-5327
Office: (800) 382-7581 (toll free)
Intake: (844) 243-8570 (toll free)
The Lafayette office serves Benton, Carroll, Cass, Clinton, Fountain, Howard, Miami, Montgomery, Tippecanoe, Tipton, Vermillion, Wabash, Warren, and White counties.

Indiana Legal Services - Merrillville
7863 Broadway Street
Suite 205
Merrillville, IN 46410
Office: 219-738-6040
Office Toll Free: (888) 255-5104
Intake Toll Free: 844-243-8570
The Merrillville office serves Jasper, Lake, Newton, and Porter counties.

Indiana Legal Services - New Albany
3303 Plaza Drive
Suite 5
New Albany, IN 47150
Office: (812) 945-4123
Office Toll Free: (800) 892-2776
Intake Toll Free: (844) 243-8570
The New Albany office serves Clark, Crawford, Dearborn, Floyd, Harrison, Jefferson, Jennings, Ohio, Ripley, Scott, Switzerland, and Washington counties.

Indiana Legal Services - Senior Law Project
151 N. Delaware
Suite 1800
Indianapolis, In 46204
Intake: (317) 631-9424
The Indianapolis Senior Law Project serves Blackford, Boone, Delaware, Fayette, Franklin, Grant, Hamilton, Hancock, Hendricks, Henry, Jay, Johnson, Marion, Madison, Morgan, Randolph, Rush, Shelby, Union, and Wayne counties.

Indiana Legal Services - South Bend
The Commerce Center
401 E. Colfax, Suite 116
South Bend, IN 46617
Office: (574) 234-8121
Office Toll Free: (800) 288-8121
Intake Toll Free: (844) 243-8570
The South Bend office serves Elkhart, Fulton, Kosciusko, LaGrange, LaPorte, Marshall, Noble, Pulaski, Starke, and St. Joseph counties.

Iowa

HELP Regional Office of Iowa Legal Aid
736 Federal Street Suite 2309
Davenport, IA 52803
1-800-532-1275

Iowa Legal Aid
1111 9th Street, Suite 230
Des Moines, IA 50314
Call toll-free 1-800-532-1275
http://www.iowalegalaid.org

Iowa Legal Aid Cedar Rapids Regional Office
317 7th Avenue SE Suite 404
Cedar Rapids, IA 52401
1-800-532-1275

Iowa Legal Aid Central Iowa Regional Office
1111 9th Street Suite 230
Des Moines, IA 50314
1-800-532-1275

Iowa Legal Aid Iowa City Regional Office
1700 South 1st Avenue Suite 10
Iowa City, IA 52240
1-800-532-1275

Iowa Legal Aid North Central Iowa Regional Office
22 North Georgia Avenue Suite 2
Mason City, IA 50401
1-800-532-1275

Iowa Legal Aid Northeast Iowa Regional Office
799 Main Street Suite 280
Dubuque, IA 52001
1-800-532-1275

Iowa Legal Aid Northwest Iowa Regional Office
507 7th St. Suite 402
Sioux City, IA 51101
1-800-532-1275

Iowa Legal Aid Southeast Iowa Regional Office
112 East 3rd Street
Ottumwa, IA 52501
1-800-532-1275

Iowa Legal Aid Southwest Iowa Regional Office
532 1st Avenue Suite 300
Council Bluffs, IA 51503
1-800-532-1275

Iowa Legal Aid Waterloo Regional Office
607 Sycamore Street Suite 304
Waterloo, IA 50703
1-800-532-1275

Legal Aid Society of Story County
937 6th Street
Nevada, IA 50201
(515) 382-2471
http://www.legalaidstory.com

Legal Hotline for Older Iowans
1111 9th Street, Suite 230
Des Moines, IA 50314
(800) 992-8161 or 992-8161 in Des Moines

Muscatine Legal Services
122 East 2nd Street
Muscatine, IA 52761
(563) 263-8663
http://muscatinelegal.com/

Kansas

Kansas Legal Services of Emporia
(620) 343-7520
527 Commercial St, Ste 201
Emporia, KS 66801
Bankruptcy, Civil Rights, Consumer and Criminal

Kansas Bar Foundation
(785) 234-5696
1200 SW Harrison St.
Topeka, KS 66612
Bankruptcy, DUI, Divorce and Elder

Kentucky

Legal Aid Society Volunteer Lawyer Program
(502) 584-1254
416 W. Muhammed Ali Blvd, Ste Fl Blvd4
Louisville, KY 40202
Bankruptcy, Civil Rights, Consumer and Criminal

Northern Kentucky Volunteer Lawyers, Inc.
(859) 431-8200
104 East Seventh Street
Covington, KY 41011
Bankruptcy, Civil Rights, Consumer and Criminal

Volunteer Lawyers for Appalachian Kentucky
(606) 886-8136
207 West Court Street, Suite 201
Prestonsburg, KY 41653
Bankruptcy, Civil Rights, Consumer and Divorce

Louisiana

Baton Rouge Bar Foundation Pro Bono Project
(225) 344-4803
544 main Street
Baton Rouge, LA 70810
Bankruptcy, Civil Rights, Consumer and Criminal

Capital Area Legal Services Contract Attorney Program
(225) 387-5173
200 3rd St
Baton Rouge, LA 70801
Bankruptcy, Civil Rights, Consumer and Criminal

Lafayette Parish Bar Association
(337) 237-4700
2607 Johnston St.
Lafayette, LA 70503
Bankruptcy, Consumer, Divorce and Education

Kisatchie Legal Services Corporation
(318) 352-7220
PO Box 1189
Natchitoches, LA 71458
Bankruptcy, Civil Rights, Consumer and Criminal

Southeast Louisiana Legal Services
(504) 529-1000
1010 Commons St.
New Orleans, LA 70403
Bankruptcy, Civil Rights, Consumer and Criminal

New Orleans Legal Assistance (an office of Southeast Louisiana Legal Services)
(504) 529-1000
1010 Common, Suite 1400A
New Orleans, LA 70112
Bankruptcy, Civil Rights, Consumer and Criminal

The Pro Bono Project
(504) 581-4043
615 Baronne Street, Suite 201
New Orleans, LA 70113
Bankruptcy, Civil Rights, Consumer and Divorce

Eighth Coast Guard District Legal Office
(504) 589-6188
501 Magazine St
New Orleans, LA 70130
Bankruptcy, Civil Rights, Consumer and Criminal

Northwest Louisiana Pro Bono Project
(318) 221-8104
625 Texas St.
Shreveport, LA 71101
Bankruptcy, Civil Rights, Divorce and Estate Planning

Maine

Upsolve
88 Federal Street
Portland, ME 04101
Bankruptcy

Maine Volunteer Lawyers Project
(800) 442-4293
75 Pearl St
Portland, ME 04112
Bankruptcy, Consumer, Divorce and Education

Maryland

Maryland, Bar Foundation, Inc. Montgomery County Pro Bono Program
(301) 424-7651
27 W Jefferson St
Rockville, MD 20850
Bankruptcy, Civil Rights, Consumer and Criminal

Maryland Volunteer Lawyers Service, Inc.
(410) 547-6537
One North Charles Street, Suite 222
Baltimore, MD 21201
Bankruptcy, Business, Consumer and Criminal

Bar Association of Baltimore City Legal Services to the Elderly Program
(410) 396-1322
111 N Calvert St, Ste 631
Baltimore, MD 21202
Bankruptcy, Consumer, Criminal and Divorce

Baltimore City Lawyer Referral and Information Service
(410) 539-3112
111 N. Calvert Street
Baltimore, MD 21202
Bankruptcy, Appeals, Collections and Consumer

Legal Aid Bureau, Inc.
(410) 539-5340
500 E Lexington St
Baltimore, MD 21202
Bankruptcy, Consumer, Criminal and Divorce

Saint Ambrose Legal Services
(410) 366-8550
321 E 25th St
Baltimore, MD 21218
Bankruptcy, Consumer and Real Estate

Massachusetts

MetroWest Legal Services
(508) 620-1830
63 Fountain Street
Framingham, MA 01702
Bankruptcy, Divorce, Education and Family

The WilmerHale Legal Services Center
(617) 522-3003
122 Boylston Street
Jamaica Plain, MA 02130
Bankruptcy, Civil Rights, Consumer and Divorce

Community Law Center
122 Boylston St
Jamaica Plain, MA 02130
Bankruptcy, Civil Rights, Consumer and Criminal

AIDS Action Committee
(617) 661-2508
1 Church Street
Cambridge, MA 02138
Bankruptcy, Civil Rights, Estate Planning and Health Care

Volunteer Lawyers Project of the Boston Bar Association
(617) 423-0648
99 Chauncy Street
Boston, MA 02111
Bankruptcy, Civil Rights, Consumer and Divorce

Volunteer Lawyers for the Arts of MA, Inc.
(617) 350-7600
15 Channel Center Street
Boston, MA 02210
Bankruptcy, Civil Rights, Consumer and Employment

Merrimack Valley Legal Services, Inc.
(978) 458-1465
35 John St, Ste Rm 302
Lowell, MA 01852
Bankruptcy, Criminal, Divorce and Family

Neighborhood Legal Services, Inc.
(781) 599-7730
181 Union Street
Lynn, MA 01901
Bankruptcy, Civil Rights, Criminal and Divorce

Legal Services for Cape Cod and Islands, Inc.
(510) 775-7020
460 W Main St
Hyannis, MA 02601
Bankruptcy, Consumer, Criminal and Divorce

Michigan

Legal Services of Northern Michigan
(906) 786-2303
806 Lundington Street
Escanaba, MI 49829
Bankruptcy, Consumer, Elder and Family

Legal Aid of Western Michigan
(616) 774-0672
25 Division Ave S, Ste 300
Grand Rapids, MI 49503
Bankruptcy, Civil Rights, Consumer and Criminal

Legal Services of Eastern Michigan
(800) 322-4512
511 Fort Street
Port Huron, MI 48060
Bankruptcy, Civil Rights, Consumer and Criminal

Elder Law of Michigan
(517) 485-9164
3815 West St. Joseph
Lansing, MI 48917
Bankruptcy, Consumer, Elder and Employment

Kalamazoo County Bar Association Legal Outreach Clinics
227 West Michigan Avenue
Kalamazoo, MI 49007
Bankruptcy, Business, Civil Rights and Consumer

Legal Services of Eastern Michigan
(800) 322-4512
436 S. Saginaw St. # 101
Flint, MI 4512
Bankruptcy, Civil Rights, Consumer and Criminal

Lakeshore Legal Aid
(888) 783-8190
30500 Van Dyke Avenue
Warren, MI 48093
Bankruptcy, Civil Rights, Consumer and Criminal

Lakeshore Legal Aid of Saint Clair County
(810) 985-5107
803 10th Ave
Port Huron, MI 48060
Bankruptcy, Civil Rights, Consumer and Divorce

Detroit Bar Association Volunteer Legal Services
(313) 961-6120
Ext. 20
645 Griswold St, Ste 3550
Detroit, MI 48226
Bankruptcy, Civil Rights, Consumer and Elder

Minnesota

Legal Aid Service of Northeastern Minnesota
(320) 629-7166
235 6th St
Pine City, MN 55063
Bankruptcy, Civil Rights, Consumer and Criminal

Volunteer Attorney Program
(320) 253-0138
830 W Saint Germain St
Saint Cloud, MN 56301
Bankruptcy, Civil Rights, Consumer and Criminal

Volunteer Attorney Program
(218) 723-4005
314 West Superior Street
Duluth, MN 55802
Bankruptcy, Civil Rights, Consumer and Criminal

Judicare of Anoka County, Inc.
(763) 783-4970
1201 89th Ave NE, Ste 310
Blaine, MN 55434
Bankruptcy, Consumer, Divorce and Employment

Central Minnesota Legal Services Volunteer Attorney Program
(612) 332-8151
430 1st Ave N, Ste 359
Minneapolis, MN 55401
Bankruptcy, Consumer, Divorce and Employment

Volunteer Lawyers Network Ltd
(612) 752-6655
600 Nicollet Mall, Ste 390A
Minneapolis, MN 55402
Bankruptcy, Civil Rights, Consumer and Divorce

Minnesota AIDS Project
(612) 341-2060
2577 W. Territorial Rd
St. Paul , MN 55114
Bankruptcy, Civil Rights, Criminal and Divorce

Southern Minnesota Regional Legal Services Volunteer Attorney Program
(507) 387-5588
12 Civic Center Plaza
Mankato, MN 56001
Bankruptcy, Civil Rights, Consumer and Criminal

Southern Minnesota Regional Legal Services Private Bar Involvement Program
(507) 372-7368
421 10th St
Worthington, MN 56187
Bankruptcy, Civil Rights, Consumer and Criminal

Legal Assistance of Olmsted County
(507) 287-2036
1700 Broadway Avenue North
Rochester, MN 55906
Bankruptcy, Consumer, Divorce and Estate Planning

Legal Services of Northwest Minnesota, Inc.
(218) 233-8585
838 Moorhead
Moorhead, MN 56561
Bankruptcy, Civil Rights, Consumer and Criminal

Mississippi

Mississippi Volunteer Lawyers Project
(601) 960-9577
1635 Lelia Dr #101
Jackson, MS 39216
Bankruptcy, Consumer, Criminal and Divorce

North Mississippi Rural Legal Services
(662) 234-2918
5 Co Rd 1014
Oxford, MS 38655
Bankruptcy, Civil Rights, Consumer and Criminal

Missouri

Mid-Missouri Legal Services Corporation
(573) 634-4545
428 East Capitol Avenue
Jefferson City, MO 65101
Bankruptcy, Consumer, Divorce and Education

Legal Services of Southern Missouri
(573) 651-4806
1225 North Kingshighway
Cape Girardeau, MO 63702-1837
Bankruptcy, Civil Rights, Consumer and Criminal

West Central Missouri Volunteer Attorney Project (WCMVAP)
(816) 474-6750
4001 Blue Parkway
Kansas City, MO 64130
Bankruptcy, Civil Rights, Consumer and Divorce

Southwest Missouri Volunteer Attorney Project (SWMVAP)
(417) 782-1650
302 S. Joplin
Joplin, MO 64801
Bankruptcy, Civil Rights, Consumer and Criminal

Northwest Missouri Volunteer Attorney Project
(816) 364-2325
PO Box 1086
Saint Joseph, MO 64502
Bankruptcy, Business, Civil Rights and Consumer

Montana

Montana Legal Services Association (MLSA) provides free civil legal help to low-income people. Contact us to see if you qualify:
- Apply anytime online at mtlsa.org;
- Call our Helpline at 1-800-666-6899 (Helpline hours are limited).

Nebraska

Nebraska State Bar Association
(402) 475-7091
PO Box 81809
Lincoln, NE 68501
Bankruptcy, Civil Rights, Consumer and Criminal

Nevada

Volunteer Attorneys for Rural Nevadans (VARN)
(775) 883-8278
904 N Nevada Street
Carson City, NV 89701
Bankruptcy, Consumer, Divorce and Estate Planning

Upsolve
530 S 6th St.
Las Vegas, NV 89101
Bankruptcy

New Hampshire

New Hampshire Pro Bono Referral System
(603) 229-0002
2 Pillsbury Street, Suite 300
Concord, NH 03301
Bankruptcy, Consumer, Criminal and Divorce

New Jersey

Mercer County Bar Association
(609) 585-6200
1245 Whitehorse Mercerville Rd, Ste 420
Hamilton, NJ 08619
Bankruptcy, Civil Rights, Consumer and Divorce

Legal Services of Northwest Jersey
(908) 782-7979
82 Park Ave
Flemington, NJ 08822
Bankruptcy, Civil Rights, Consumer and Divorce

Central Jersey Legal Services
(732) 249-7600
317 George St.
New Brunswick, NJ 08901
Bankruptcy, Divorce, Education and Employment

South Jersey Legal Services
(888) 576-5529
PO Box 1357
Edison, NJ 08818
Bankruptcy, Consumer, Criminal and Divorce

Union County Legal Services Corporation
(908) 354-4340
60 Prince St
Elizabeth, NJ 07208
Bankruptcy, Civil Rights, Consumer and Criminal

Volunteer Lawyers for Justice
(973) 645-1955
P.O. Box 32040
Newark, NJ 07102
Bankruptcy, Consumer, Criminal and Divorce

Rutgers School of Law Urban Legal Clinic
(973) 353-5576
123 Washington Street
Newark, NJ 07102
Bankruptcy, Consumer, Criminal and Divorce

Upsolve
1300 Atlantic Avenue
Atlantic City, NJ 08401
Bankruptcy

Northeast New Jersey Legal Services
(201) 792-6363
574 Summit Avenue
Jersey City, NJ 07306
Bankruptcy, Civil Rights, Consumer and Criminal

New Mexico

Legal Aid Society Of Albuquerque Pro Bono Project
(866) 416-1922
301 Gold Ave. SW,
Albuquerque, NM 87102
Bankruptcy, Criminal, Divorce and Family

Legal Resources for the Elderly Program (LREP)
(800) 876-6657
PO Box 92860
Albuquerque, NM 87199
Bankruptcy, Collections, Consumer and Foreclosure Defense

New York

Legal Aid Society of Mid-New York, Inc.
(315) 793-7000
268 Genesee St
Utica, NY 13502
Bankruptcy, Civil Rights, Consumer and Criminal

Law Assistance of Western New York
(315) 781-1465
361 South Main Street
Geneva, NY 14456
Bankruptcy, Consumer, Domestic Violence and Family

Empire Justice Center
(585) 454-4060
1 West Main Street
Rochester, NY 14614
Bankruptcy, Civil Rights, Consumer and Education

Volunteer Legal Services Project of Monroe County, Inc.
(585) 232-3051
1 West Main St.
Rochester, NY 14614
Bankruptcy, Civil Rights, Consumer and Criminal

The Legal Project
(518) 435-1770
24 Aviation Road, Suite 101
Albany, NY 12203
Bankruptcy, Civil Rights, Consumer and Criminal

Legal Aid Society of Northeastern New York, Inc.
(518) 462-6765
55 Colvin Ave
Albany, NY 12206
Bankruptcy, Consumer, Criminal and Divorce

Erie County Bar Association Volunteer Lawyers Project
(716) 852-8687
438 Main Street (Sixth Floor)
Buffalo, NY 14202
Bankruptcy, Business, Civil Rights and Consumer

Western New York Law Center
(716) 855-0203
237 Main Street
Buffalo, NY 14203
Bankruptcy, Civil Rights, Consumer and Elder

African Services Committee
(212) 222-3882
429 West 127th Street
New York, NY 10027
Bankruptcy, Civil Rights, Employment and Estate Planning

Volunteer Lawyers for the Arts - New York
(212) 319-2787
1 E 53rd St, Ste Fl 6
New York, NY 10022
Bankruptcy, Business, Civil Rights and Consumer

City Bar Justice Center
(212) 382-6600
42 West 44th Street
New York, NY 10036
Bankruptcy, Divorce, Domestic Violence and Family

New York City Financial Justice Hotline
(212) 925-4929
121 West 27th Street
New York, NY 10001
Bankruptcy and Tax

Gay Men's Health Crisis Legal Services & Advocacy Dept.
(212) 367-1040
119 W 24th St
New York, NY 10011
Bankruptcy, Civil Rights, Consumer and Divorce

Bet Tzedek Legal Services Clinic at Cardozo School of Law
(212) 790-0240
55 Fifth Avenue
New York, NY 10003
Bankruptcy, Civil Rights, Consumer and Education

New York County Lawyers' Association
(212) 267-6646
14 Vessey Street
New York, NY 10007
Bankruptcy, Consumer, Divorce and Employment

New York County Lawyers' Association
(212) 267-6646
Ext. 217
14 Vesey St
New York, NY 10007
Bankruptcy, Consumer, Divorce and Employment

MFY Legal Services
(212) 417-3700
100 William Street, 6th Floor
New York, NY 10038
Bankruptcy, Consumer, Elder and Employment

Brooklyn Bar Association Volunteer Lawyers Project, Inc.
(718) 624-3894
123 Remsen St
Brooklyn, NY 11201
Bankruptcy, Civil Rights, Consumer and Criminal

BLS Legal Services Corporation Senior Citizens Law Office
(718) 488-7448
1 Boerum Pl, Ste Fl 3
Brooklyn, NY 11201
Bankruptcy, Consumer, Estate Planning and Real Estate

Upsolve
(347) 850-2656
150 Court St.
Brooklyn, NY 11201
Bankruptcy

HIV Law Project
(212) 577-3001
81 Willoughby Street, 5th Floor.
New York, NY 10038
Bankruptcy, Consumer, Employment and Estate Planning

Queens Volunteer Lawyers Project, Inc.
(718) 739-4100
9035 148th St
Jamaica, NY 11435
Bankruptcy, Consumer, Divorce and Estate Planning

AIDS Center of Queens County (ACQC)
(718) 896-2500
161-21 Jamaica Ave
Jamaica, NY 11432
Bankruptcy, Civil Rights, Consumer and Criminal

FILE BANKRUPTCY FOR FREE

North Country Legal Services
(518) 563-4022
PO Box 989
Plattsburgh, NY 12901
Bankruptcy, Consumer, Divorce and Estate Planning

Long Island Association for AIDS Care
(631) 385-2451
60 Adams Ave.
Hauppauge, NY 11788
Bankruptcy, Civil Rights, Estate Planning and Health Care

North Carolina

Legal Services of Southern Piedmont, Inc.
(704) 376-1600
1431 Elizabeth Ave
Charlotte, NC 28204
Bankruptcy, Consumer, Criminal and Divorce

Legal Services of Mecklenburg County, NC
(704) 376-1600
1431 Elizabeth Ave
Charlotte, NC 28204
Bankruptcy, Civil Rights, Consumer and Criminal

Mecklenburg County Bar Association
(704) 375-8624
2850 Zebulon Avenue
Charlotte, NC 28208
Bankruptcy, Civil Rights, Consumer and Criminal

Land Loss Prevention Project, Inc.
(800) 672-5839
PO Box 179
Durham, NC 27702
Bankruptcy, Business, Civil Rights and Consumer

Blue Ridge Area Volunteer Lawyers Program
(704) 264-5640
171 Grand Blvd
Boone, NC 28607
Bankruptcy, Consumer, Criminal and Divorce

Pisgah Legal Services Mountain Area Volunteer Lawyers (MAVL) Administered
(828) 253-0406
89 Montford Ave
Asheville, NC 28801
Bankruptcy, Civil Rights, Consumer and Criminal

Legal Services of the Coastal Plains
(919) 332-5124
610 Church St E
Ahoskie, NC 27910
Bankruptcy, Civil Rights, Consumer and Criminal

North Dakota

North Dakota State Bar Association LRS
(701) 255-1404
1661 Capitol Way, Suite 104LL
Bismarck, ND 58501
Bankruptcy, Divorce, Elder and Family

Ohio

Southeastern Ohio Legal Services
(740) 773-0012
73 East Water Street
Chillicothe, OH 45601
Bankruptcy, Civil Rights, Consumer and Divorce

Community Legal Aid Services, Inc.
(330) 456-8361
306 Market Avenue N.,
Canton, OH 44702
Bankruptcy, Consumer, Criminal and Divorce

Legal Aid of Greater Cincinnati
10 Journal Square
Hamilton, OH 45011
Bankruptcy, Civil Rights, Consumer and Criminal

Greater Dayton Volunteer Lawyers Project
(937) 461-3857
109 N. Main Street Suite 610
Dayton, OH 45402
Bankruptcy, Civil Rights, Consumer and Criminal

Advocates for Basic Legal Equality, Inc. (ABLE)
(800) 837-0814
1340 W. High St., Suite A
Defiance, OH 43512
Bankruptcy, Civil Rights, Criminal and Divorce

Legal Aid Society of Cleveland
1223 W 6th St
Cleveland, OH 44113
Bankruptcy, Civil Rights, Consumer and Criminal

Cleveland Homeless Legal Assistance Program
(216) 696-3525
1375 E. 9th St. Floor 2
Cleveland, OH 44114
Bankruptcy and Real Estate

Northeast Ohio Legal Services
(330) 744-3196
11 Federal Plaza Central
Youngstown, OH 44503
Bankruptcy, Civil Rights, Consumer and Criminal

Pro Seniors, Inc.
(513) 345-4160
105 E 4th St, Ste 1715
Cincinnati, OH 45202
Bankruptcy, Civil Rights, Consumer and Divorce

Oklahoma

Legal Aid Services of Oklahoma Inc.
(405) 557-0020
2915 N Classen Blvd, Ste 500
Oklahoma City, OK 73106
Bankruptcy, Civil Rights, Consumer and Criminal

Oregon

Albany Regional Office - Legal Aid Services of Oregon
433 Fourth Ave. SW
Albany, OR 97321
(541) 926-8678

Center for Non-Profit Legal Services
225 W. Main Street
Medford, OR 97501
(541) 779-7291

Central Oregon Regional Office - Legal Aid Services of Oregon
42 NW Greeley Avenue
Bend, OR 97703
(541) 385-6950

Columbia County Office of Oregon Law Center
270 South First St.
St. Helens, OR 97051
(503) 397-1628
http://oregonlawcenter.org/how-to-get-help/olc-offices/hillsboro/

Coos Bay Office - Oregon Law Center
455 S. 4th Street, Suite 5
Coos Bay, OR 97420
(541) 269-1226, 1-800-303-3638
http://oregonlawcenter.org/how-to-get-help/olc-offices/coos-bay/

Grants Pass Office - Oregon Law Center
424 NW 6th Street, Suite 102
PO Box 429
Grants Pass, OR 97528
(541) 476-1058
http://oregonlawcenter.org/how-to-get-help/olc-offices/grants-pass/

Hillsboro Regional Office - Oregon Law Center
230 N.E. Second Ave., Suite F
Hillsboro, OR 97124
503-640-4115; 1-877-296-4076 (Toll-Free)
http://oregonlawcenter.org/how-to-get-help/olc-offices/hillsboro/

Klamath Falls Regional Office - Legal Aid Services of Oregon
832 Klamath Avenue
Klamath Falls, OR 97601
(541) 273-0533

Lane County Legal Aid/OLC
376 E. Eleventh Street
Eugene, OR 97401
(541) 485-1017, 1-800-575-9283
http://www.lclac.org/

Legal Aid Services of Oregon - Central Administrative Office
520 SW Sixth Avenue
Suite 1130
Portland, OR 97204
(503) 224-4094

Lincoln County Office - Legal Aid Services of Oregon
304 SW Coast Highway
Newport, OR 97365
(541) 265-5305
(800) 222-3884

McMinnville Office - Oregon Law Center
The Eagle Building, 117 NE 5th Street
Suite B
McMinnville, OR 97128
(503) 472-9561
http://oregonlawcenter.org/how-to-get-help/olc-offices/mcminnville/

Native American Program - Legal Aid Services of Oregon
4531 SE Belmont Street
Suite 201
Portland, OR 97215
(503) 223-9483

Ontario Office - Oregon Law Center
35 SE 5th Avenue, Unit #1
Ontario, OR 97914
(541) 889-3121
(888) 250-9877
http://oregonlawcenter.org/how-to-get-help/olc-offices/ontario/

Oregon Law Center - Salem
494 State Street, Suite 410
Salem, OR 97301
(503) 485-0696
(888) 601-7907
http://oregonlawcenter.org/how-to-get-help/olc-offices/salem/

Pendleton Regional Office - Legal Aid Services of Oregon
365 SE 3rd Street
Pendleton, OR 97801
(541) 276-6685
(800) 843-1115

Portland Office - Oregon Law Center
522 SW Fifth Avenue, Suite 812
Portland, OR 97204
http://oregonlawcenter.org/how-to-get-help/olc-offices/portland/

Portland Regional Office - Legal Aid Services of Oregon
520 SW 6th Avenue
Suite 700
Portland, OR 97204
(503) 224-4086
1-800-228-6958 Toll-Free

Roseburg Office - Legal Aid Services of Oregon
700 SE Kane Street
Roseburg, OR 97470
(541) 673-1181
1-888-668-9406 (toll free)

Salem Regional Office - Legal Aid Services of Oregon
105 High Street SE
Salem, OR 97301
(503) 581-5265
(800) 359-1845

Senior Law Project
520 SW 6th Avenue
Suite 700
Portland, OR 97204
https://lasoregon.org

St. Andrew Legal Clinic, Multnomah Co.
807 NE Alberta St.
Portland, OR 97211
503-281-1500
http://www.salcgroup.org/

St. Andrew Legal Clinic, Washington & Columbia Counties
232 NE Lincoln St., Suite H
Hillsboro, OR 97124
503-648-1600
http://www.salcgroup.org/

Pennsylvania

Mid-Penn Legal Services
(717) 234-0492
213-A N. Front St.
Harrisburg, PA 17101
Bankruptcy, Civil Rights, Consumer and Criminal

Dauphin County Bar Association
(717) 232-7536
213 N Front St
Harrisburg, PA 17101
Bankruptcy, Consumer, Criminal and Divorce

Pennsylvania Legal Aid Network
(717) 236-9486
118 Locust Street
Harrisburg, PA 17101
Bankruptcy, Civil Rights, Consumer and Domestic Violence

YWCA of Harrisburg Domestic Violence Legal Center
(717) 724-0516
112 Market St., 4th Floor
Harrisburg, PA 17101
Bankruptcy, Consumer, Divorce and Domestic Violence

Luzerne County Pro Bono Project for the Elderly
(570) 825-8567
15 Public Sq, Ste 410
Wilkes Barre, PA 18701
Bankruptcy

Chester County Bar Association Access to Justice
(610) 692-1889
15 West Gay Street
West Chester, PA 19380
Bankruptcy, Divorce, Elder and Estate Planning

Neighborhood Legal Services Association
(724) 282-3888
(Not a Physical Office Location)
Butler, PA 16101
Bankruptcy, Divorce, Elder and Family

Upsolve
718 Arch Street Suite 300N
Philadelphia, PA 19106
Bankruptcy

Legal Aid of Southeastern Pennsylvania
(877) 429-5994
Norristown, PA 19401
Bankruptcy, Consumer, Criminal and Divorce

Community Legal Services of Philadelphia
(215) 981-3700
1424 Chestnut Street
Philadelphia, PA 19102
Bankruptcy, Business, Consumer and Elder

Philadelphia Volunteer Lawyers for the Arts
(215) 790-3620
200 South Broad Street
Philadelphia, PA 19102
Bankruptcy, Business, Civil Rights and Consumer

AIDS Law Project of Pennsylvania
(215) 587-9377
1211 Chestnut St, Ste 600
Philadelphia, PA 19107
Bankruptcy, Civil Rights, Consumer and Criminal

Legal Aid Volunteer Attorneys (LAVA)
(814) 452-6957
1001 State Street
Erie, PA 16501
Bankruptcy, Civil Rights, Consumer and Divorce

Northwestern Legal Services
1001 State St, Ste 1200
Erie, PA 16501
Bankruptcy, Divorce, Employment and Estate Planning

Rhode Island

Rhode Island Bar Association
(401) 421-5740
41 Sharpe Dr.
Cranston, RI 02920
Bankruptcy, Business, Civil Rights and Consumer

South Carolina

South Carolina Bar Association Pro Bono Program
950 Taylor Street
Columbia, SC 29202
Bankruptcy, Civil Rights, Consumer and Criminal

South Dakota
Dakota Plains Legal Service

Mission Office
605-856-4444
Toll Free
800-658-2297

Rapid City Office
605-342-7171
Toll Free
800-742-8602

Pine Ridge Office
605-867-1020
Sisseton Office
605-698-3971

Eagle Butte Office
605-964-2175

Ft. Yates Office
701-854-7204

Ft. Thompson Office
605-245-2341

Tennessee

Legal Aid Society of Middle Tennessee Inc Williamson County Pro Bono Program
(615) 890-0905
526 N Walnut St
Murfreesboro, TN 37130
Bankruptcy, Consumer, Criminal and Divorce

Knoxville Legal Aid Society, Inc. Pro Bono Project
(423) 525-3425
502 S Gay St, Ste 404
Knoxville, TN 37902
Bankruptcy, Civil Rights, Consumer and Divorce

Texas

AIDS Services of Austin
(512) 458-2437
P.O. Box 4874
Austin, TX 78765
Bankruptcy, Civil Rights, Consumer and Criminal

San Antonio Bar Association Community Justice Program
(210) 227-8822
100 Dolorosa
San Antonio, TX 78205
Bankruptcy, Consumer, Employment and Estate Planning

Volunteer Legal Services of Central Texas
(512) 476-5550
1033 La Posada Drive, Suite 374
Austin, TX 78752
Bankruptcy, Consumer, Divorce and Elder

Tarrant County Bar Association Legal Line
(817) 335-1239
1315 Calhoun Street
Fort Worth, TX 76102
Bankruptcy, Civil Rights, Consumer and Divorce

Legal Aid of Northwest Texas Bankruptcy Law Clinic
(817) 336-3943
600 East Weatherford St.
Fort Worth, TX 76102
Bankruptcy

Dallas Volunteer Attorney Program
(214) 243-2236
1515 Main Street
Dallas, TX 75201
Bankruptcy, Civil Rights, Consumer and Divorce

Dallas Bar Association LegalLine
(214) 220-7476
2101 Ross Avenue
Dallas, TX 75201
Bankruptcy, Civil Rights, Consumer and Criminal

Houston Bar Association LegalLine
(713) 759-1133
1111 Bagby St., FLB 200
Houston, TX 77002
Bankruptcy, Civil Rights, Consumer and Divorce

Houston Volunteer Lawyer Program
(713) 228-0735
1111 Bagby
Houston, TX 77002
Bankruptcy, Consumer, Divorce and Domestic Violence

Consejos Legales
(713) 759-1133
1001 Fannin Street
Houston, TX 77002
Bankruptcy, Civil Rights, Consumer and Divorce

University of Houston Law Civil Practice Clinic
(713) 743-2100
4604 Calhoun Road
Houston, TX 77204
Bankruptcy, Divorce, Domestic Violence and Estate Planning

Jefferson County Pro Bono Program
(409) 839-2332
1001 Pearl
Beaumont, TX 77701
Bankruptcy, Consumer, Divorce and Employment

Utah
Utah Legal Services

Salt Lake City
Address: 205 N 400 W Salt Lake City, UT 84103 (get Directions)
Phone: (801) 328-8891
Fax: (801) 869-2715
Contact: Mary Lyman

Provo
Address: 455 N University Ave, Ste. 100, Provo, UT 84601 (get Directions)
Phone: (801) 374-6766
Fax: (801) 655-5350
Contact: Sharon White

Ogden
Address: 298 24th St, Ste. 110, Ogden, UT 84401 (get Directions)
Phone: (801) 394-9431
Fax: (801) 827-0420
Contact: Gary Anderson

St. George
Address: 229 St George Blvd, Ste. 103, St George, UT 84770 (get Directions)
Phone: (435) 628-1604
Fax: (435) 986-7163
Contact: Eric Mittelstadt

Vermont
Vermont Legal Aid

Burlington
264 North Winooski Avenue | Burlington VT 05401
Phone: 802.863.5620 | Fax: 802.863.7152

Montpelier
56 College Street | Montpelier VT 05602
Phone: 802.223.6377 | Fax: 802.223.7281

Rutland
57 North Main Street, Suite 2 | Rutland VT 05701
Phone: 802.775.0021 | Fax: 802.775.0022

Springfield
56 Main Street, Suite 301 | Springfield VT 05156
Phone: 802.885.5181 | Fax: 802.885.5754

St. Johnsbury
177 Western Avenue, Suite 1 | St. Johnsbury VT 05819
Phone: 802.748.8721 | Fax: 802.748.4610

Virginia
Virginia Legal Aid Society

Lynchburg Office
513 Church Street
Lynchburg, VA 24504
Phone: 434-846-1326

Danville Office
519 Main Street
Danville, VA 24541
Phone: 434-799-3550

© BE Adviser

Suffolk Office
155 E. Washington St.
Suffolk, VA 23434
Phone: 757-539-3441

Farmville Office
217 East Third Street
Farmville, VA 23901
Phone: 434-392-8108

Central Virginia Legal Aid Society

CHARLOTTESVILLE OFFICE
1000 Preston Avenue, Suite B,
Charlottesville, VA 22903
434-296-8851
toll-free 800-390-9982

RICHMOND OFFICE
101 West Broad Street, Suite 101
Richmond, VA 23220
804-648-1012
toll-free 800-868-1012

PETERSBURG OFFICE
229 North Sycamore Street
Petersburg, VA 23803
804-862-1100
toll-free 800-868-1012

Legal Services of Northern Virginia

Alexandria Office
100 N. Pitt Street, Suite 307
Alexandria, VA 22314

Arlington Office
3401 Columbia Pike, Suite 301
Arlington, VA 22204

Fairfax Office
10700 Page Avenue, Suite 100
Fairfax, VA 22030

Fredericksburg Office
500 Lafayette Blvd, Suite 140
Fredericksburg, VA 22401

Loudoun Office
8A South Street, SW
Leesburg, VA 20175

Prince William Office
9240 Center Street
Manassas, VA 20110

Route 1 Office
8305 Richmond Highway, Suite 17B
Alexandria, VA 22309

Washington

Upsolve
1104 Main Street
Vancouver, WA 98660
Bankruptcy

West Virginia
Legal Aid of West Virginia

Charleston
922 Quarrier St., 4th Floor
Charleston, WV 25301

Beckley
115B South Kanawha Street
Beckley, WV 25801

Clarksburg
110 South Third Street
Clarksburg, WV 26301

Elkins
224 Third Street, PO Box 229
Elkins, WV 26241

Huntington
418 8th Street, Second Floor
Huntington, WV 25701

Lewisburg
125 Green Lane
Lewisburg, WV 24901

Logan
107 Stratton Street
Logan, WV 25601

Martinsburg
301 W. Burke St., Suite B
Martinsburg, WV 25401

Morgantown
165 Scott Avenue, Suite 209
Morgantown, WV 26508

Parkersburg
327 Ninth Street
Parkersburg, WV 26101

Princeton
1519 North Walker Street
Princeton, WV 24740

Wheeling
The Mull Center, 1025 Main Street, Suite 716,
Wheeling, WV 26003

Wisconsin

Legal Action of Wisconsin - Madison Area Office
(608) 256-3304
744 Williamson Street, Ste. 200
Madison, WI 53703
Bankruptcy, Civil Rights, Consumer and Criminal

Legal Action of Wisconsin - Milwaukee & Waukesha Office
(855) 947-2527
230 W Wells St, Ste 800
Milwaukee, WI 53203
Bankruptcy, Civil Rights, Consumer and Criminal

Wyoming
Legal Aid of Wyoming

Cody Office
1001 14th Street, Ste. A
Cody, WY 82414
Toll Free: 1-877-432-9955

Gillette Office
400 S. Kendrick, Ste. 304
Gillette, WY 82716
Telephone: 1-307-459-5765

Casper Office
159 North Wolcott Street, Ste 100
Casper, WY 82601
Telephone: 307-232-9827

Lander Office
420 Lincoln Street
Lander, WY 82520
Telephone: 307-332-3517

Rock Springs Office
2620 Commercial Way Ste. 5
Rock Springs WY 82901
Telephone: 307-459-5764

Washington, DC

American Association Of Retired Persons Legal Counsel For The Elderly Volunteer LawyersProject
(202) 434-2120
601 E St NW, Ste Fl 4
Washington, DC 20049
Bankruptcy, Civil Rights, Consumer and Divorce

DC Bar Pro Bono Program
(202) 626-3499
1250 H St NW, 6th Floor
Washington, DC 20005
Bankruptcy, Civil Rights, Consumer and Criminal

Upsolve
718 Arch Street Suite 300N
Philadelphia, PA 19106
Bankruptcy

APPENDIX B

Links to Court Websites
(Retrieved from https://www.uscourts.gov/about-federal-courts/federal-courts-public/court-website-links)

U.S. Bankruptcy Courts

Alabama Middle
https://www.almb.uscourts.gov/
Alabama Northern
https://www.alnb.uscourts.gov/
Alabama Southern
https://www.alsb.uscourts.gov/

Alaska
https://www.akb.uscourts.gov/

Arizona
http://www.azb.uscourts.gov/

Arkansas Eastern & Western
https://www.areb.uscourts.gov/

California Central
https://www.cacb.uscourts.gov/
California Eastern
http://www.caeb.uscourts.gov/
California Northern
http://www.canb.uscourts.gov/
California Southern
https://www.casb.uscourts.gov/

Colorado
https://www.cob.uscourts.gov/

Connecticut
https://www.ctb.uscourts.gov/

Delaware
http://www.deb.uscourts.gov/

U.S. Bankruptcy Courts

District of Columbia
https://www.dcb.uscourts.gov

Florida Middle
http://www.flmb.uscourts.gov/
Florida Northern
http://www.flnb.uscourts.gov/
Florida Southern
https://www.flsb.uscourts.gov

Georgia Middle
http://www.gamb.uscourts.gov/USCourts/
Georgia Northern
http://www.ganb.uscourts.gov/
Georgia Southern
https://www.gasb.uscourts.gov

Guam
http://www.gud.uscourts.gov/

Hawaii
http://www.hib.uscourts.gov/

Idaho
http://www.id.uscourts.gov/clerks/Welcome.cfm?

Illinois Central
https://www.ilcb.uscourts.gov/
Illinois Northern
https://www.ilnb.uscourts.gov/
Illinois Southern
www.ilsb.uscourts.gov
Indiana Northern
https://www.innb.uscourts.gov/

Indiana Southern
https://www.insb.uscourts.gov/
Iowa Northern
http://www.ianb.uscourts.gov/publicweb/

Iowa Southern
https://www.iasb.uscourts.gov/

Kansas
https://www.ksb.uscourts.gov/

Kentucky Eastern
https://www.kyeb.uscourts.gov/

U.S. Bankruptcy Courts

Kentucky Western
http://www.kywb.uscourts.gov/fpweb/index.htm

Louisiana Eastern
https://www.laeb.uscourts.gov/

Louisiana Middle
https://www.lamb.uscourts.gov/

Louisiana Western
https://www.lawb.uscourts.gov/

Maine
http://www.meb.uscourts.gov/

Maryland
https://www.mdb.uscourts.gov/

Massachusetts
http://www.mab.uscourts.gov/mab/

Michigan Eastern
http://www.mieb.uscourts.gov/
Michigan Western
https://www.miwb.uscourts.gov/

Minnesota
https://www.mnb.uscourts.gov/

Mississippi Northern
https://www.msnb.uscourts.gov/
Mississippi Southern
http://www.mssb.uscourts.gov/

Missouri Eastern
https://www.moeb.uscourts.gov/
Missouri Western
https://www.mow.uscourts.gov/

Montana
https://www.mtb.uscourts.gov/

Nebraska
https://www.neb.uscourts.gov/

U.S. Bankruptcy Courts

Nevada
https://www.nvb.uscourts.gov/

New Hampshire
https://www.nhb.uscourts.gov/

New Jersey
http://www.njb.uscourts.gov/

New Mexico
http://www.nmb.uscourts.gov/

New York Eastern
https://www.nyeb.uscourts.gov/
New York Northern
http://www.nynb.uscourts.gov/
New York Southern
http://www.nysb.uscourts.gov/
New York Western
https://www.nywb.uscourts.gov/

North Carolina Eastern
https://www.nceb.uscourts.gov/
North Carolina Middle
http://www.ncmb.uscourts.gov/
North Carolina Western
https://www.ncwb.uscourts.gov/

North Dakota
http://www.ndb.uscourts.gov/

Northern Mariana Islands
http://www.nmid.uscourts.gov/

Ohio Northern
https://www.ohnb.uscourts.gov/
Ohio Southern
https://www.ohsb.uscourts.gov/

Oklahoma Eastern
http://www.okeb.uscourts.gov/
Oklahoma Northern
http://www.oknb.uscourts.gov/
Oklahoma Western
https://www.okwb.uscourts.gov/

U.S. Bankruptcy Courts

Oregon
https://www.orb.uscourts.gov/

Pennsylvania Eastern
https://www.paeb.uscourts.gov/
Pennsylvania Middle
http://www.pamb.uscourts.gov/
Pennsylvania Western
http://www.pawb.uscourts.gov/

Puerto Rico
http://www.prb.uscourts.gov/

Rhode Island
http://www.rib.uscourts.gov/

South Carolina
http://www.scb.uscourts.gov/
South Dakota
https://www.sdb.uscourts.gov/

Tennessee Eastern
http://www.tneb.uscourts.gov/
Tennessee Middle
http://www.tnmb.uscourts.gov/
Tennessee Western
http://www.tnwb.uscourts.gov/TNW/index.aspx

Texas Eastern
https://www.txeb.uscourts.gov/
Texas Northern
https://www.txnb.uscourts.gov/
Texas Southern
https://www.txs.uscourts.gov/page/bankruptcy-court
Texas Western
https://www.txwb.uscourts.gov/

Utah
https://www.utb.uscourts.gov/

Vermont
https://www.vtb.uscourts.gov/

Virgin Islands
https://www.vid.uscourts.gov/bankruptcy-division

U.S. Bankruptcy Courts

Virginia Eastern
https://www.vaeb.uscourts.gov/wordpress/
Virginia Western
http://www.vawb.uscourts.gov/

Washington Eastern
https://www.waeb.uscourts.gov/
Washington Western
http://www.wawb.uscourts.gov/

West Virginia Northern
https://www.wvnb.uscourts.gov/
West Virginia Southern
https://www.wvsb.uscourts.gov/
Wisconsin Eastern
https://www.wieb.uscourts.gov/

Wisconsin Western
https://www.wiwb.uscourts.gov/

Wyoming
https://www.wyb.uscourts.gov/